How to Succeed in

INTERMEDIATE LEVEL

BUSINESS GNVQs

Sanjay Modha

GW00727969

First published in 1997

Apart from any fair dealing for the purposes of research or private study, or criticism or review, as permitted under the Copyright, Designs and Patents Act 1988, this publication may only be reproduced, stored or transmitted, in any form or by any means, with the prior permission in writing of the publishers, or in the case of reprographic reproduction in accordance with the terms of licences issued by the Copyright Licensing Agency. Enquiries concerning reproduction outside those terms should be sent to the publishers at the undermentioned address:

Kogan Page Limited
120 Pentonville Road
London N1 9JN

© Sanjay Modha, 1997

British Library Cataloguing in Publication Data

A CIP record for this book is available from the British Library.

ISBN 0 7494 2215 7

Typeset by JS Typesetting, Wellingborough, Northants
Printed and bound in Great Britain by Clays Ltd, St Ives plc

Contents

Chapter 1
Background to GNVQ Tests

Introduction

The idea for this book arose from the lack of a text for GNVQ Business (intermediate level) covering all tests that students could use to practise, prior to taking an exam.

Its aim is to make available to a wider audience the strategies developed while preparing candidates for GNVQ tests. Its primary purpose is to assist students in preparing for these tests. What is provided is a set of five tests for each of the units that are externally tested.

Most people dread the thought of taking a test or an exam. Tests or exams are seen as an obstacle and therefore many candidates approach them in a negative frame of mind rather than a positive outlook; they should view the tests as an opportunity to demonstrate their knowledge and understanding of the subject matter.

Practice can result in significant improvements in performance. It also boosts confidence and helps individuals to cope with anxiety. This is important, as anxiety can distract one's full attention from the task in hand – that of taking a test.

Practice also makes individuals less likely to make mistakes and ensures that the test is approached proficiently.

What is a GNVQ?

GNVQs (General National Vocational Qualifications) are nationally recognised qualifications. Currently, three awarding bodies offer GNVQs, namely BTEC, RSA and City and Guilds. They offer a wide range of subjects including Business Studies. There are three levels at which GNVQ Business is being offered. They are Foundation, Intermediate and Advanced. The advanced level is the equivalent of two A levels. Hence this fulfils the minimum entry requirement for a university place. Further information about specific subjects can be obtained from colleges of further education or directly from the awarding bodies themselves.

To successfully achieve the intermediate (Level 2) GNVQ in Business it is necessary to complete nine units. These consist of:

- 4 mandatory units (listed below)
- 3 key skills units (core skills); these are:
  Application of number
  Communication
  Information technology
- 2 optional units (these have not been listed here because they will vary from one awarding body to another).

The body set up by the government to oversee the development of GNVQs is called the National Council for Vocational Qualifications or NCVQ.

When you have completed and passed your GNVQs at Level 2 you can then progress to study for the advanced level.

The GNVQs have three levels of grading. These are:

- Pass
- Merit
- Distinction

The distinction grade is the highest level at which you can pass the course and the pass grade is the lowest.

What is tested?

GNVQ Business (intermediate level) has four core units, of which three are subject to external testing. **Unit four** – Financial and Administrative Support – is not tested by an external exam but is assessed by means of assignments and project work. The three units are as follows:

Unit One   Business Organisations and Employment
Unit Two   People in Business Organisations
Unit Three   Consumers and Customers

For test purposes each unit is divided into a number of 'focus' areas. This means that a particular aspect of the unit is tested in that focus area. For example, in Unit Two – People in Business

Organisations, focus three is job roles within business organisations, so the questions would relate to this aspect.

Example

Which of the following would a production manager be most concerned with?

    A   day-to-day functioning of the company
    B   the grievances currently outstanding
    C   strategic planning
    D   the production targets for the next two months

The units are divided equally in terms of focus areas; each unit has three focus areas as follows:

Unit One	**Business Organisations and Employment**
Focus one	Purposes and types of business organisations
Focus two	Business location, environment and products
Focus three	Types of employment
Unit Two	**People in Business Organisations**
Focus one	Organisational structures and working arrangements
Focus two	Employee and employer rights and responsibilities
Focus three	Job roles within business organisations
Unit three	**Consumers and Customers**
Focus one	Importance of consumers and customers
Focus two	Types of promotion in business
Focus three	Providing customer service

Question formats

Format 1

A question is asked or a statement is made. This is then followed by four answer choices, lettered A to D. You would then choose one of the letters: A, B, C or D.

Example

Which of the following departments would be involved in the recruitment process?

A	operations	C	accounts
B	personnel	D	marketing

Format 2

Layout 1

Here you are given two statements, each of which is true or false. You then have to choose one answer from the four choices that apply to those statements.

A True True – this is where both statements are true
B True False – this is where the first statement is true and the second is false
C False True – you would choose this if the first is false but the second is true
D False False – where both statements are false.

Example

Say whether each of the following statements is T (true) or F (false).

Statement 1
An advantage of using a computerised database is that information can be retrieved quickly.

Statement 2
A problem with computerised databases is that information cannot be updated easily.

A	True	True	C	False	True
B	True	False	D	False	False

Layout 2

As with Layout 1, you are given two statements and each one is either true or false; you have to choose from the four alternatives that are offered.

A   i) T ii) T – both statements are true
B   i) T ii) F – first statement is true, the second is false
C   i) F ii) T – first statement is false, the second is true
D   i) F ii) F – both statements are false.

Example

Say whether each of the following statements is T (true) or F (false).

Statement 1
The Sex Discrimination Act applies to women only.

Statement 2
Men can be discriminated against on the grounds of sex because the Act does not apply to them.

A	i) T ii) T	C	i) F ii) T
B	i) T ii) F	D	i) F ii) F

Format 3

A statement is made or a question is asked and you are presented with four possible answers of which two are correct. You are then to choose the two which are correct.

i   _____
ii   _____
iii _____
iv _____

A	i) & ii)	C	i) & iv)
B	ii) & iii)	D	ii) & iv)

Example

It would be discriminatory to ask two of the following questions. Which two?

(i)   *Would you be able to cope with the work load?*
(ii)   *As a woman, are you planning to have children?*
(iii) *What experience have you had of this type of work?*
(iv) *As a mother, what child care provisions have you made?*

A	i) and ii)	C	ii) and iii)
B	i) and iii)	D	ii) and iv)

Format 4

Here you are given four options such as names of departments in an organisation. You are then asked several questions and are to select the answer from the four options.

Example

A supermarket uses the following methods of communication:

A	*telephone*	C	*electronic mail (e-mail)*
B	*facsimile*	D	*notice boards*

Which methods should be used for:

1 *Leaving a confidential message when the recipient is away from the office?*

   A   B   C   D

2 *Keeping sales assistants informed of general company matters?*

   A   B   C   D

3 *An urgent but confidential message, requiring immediate action?*

   A   B   C   D

Why practise?

Supposing you have been asked to take part in a hurdles race. What would you do? You wouldn't simply turn up on the day and hope that you would be able to complete the race (let alone win it) and not fall over at the first hurdle.

What you would do is to start training for the race – that is, practise. So why should preparing for a test be different? The same principle applies: you have to practise to learn how to jump over the hurdles without falling over.

The fact is that it is very difficult to sit down to study alone. It takes a lot of effort and self-discipline to force yourself to concentrate, particularly when the subject matter is difficult to understand. The whole process of studying becomes boring. Studying is a skill. If you don't have the right study skills you must do something to acquire them.

If you take just a few minutes to think about the last time you were planning to sit down to do some studying, what happened?

There you were thinking 'Right, I'm going to make a start on that assignment or project'. As you sat there, the television was on, showing a boring documentary or a discussion programme. So you thought, 'Let me just see what it's about' and it became interesting (and you promised yourself that you would only watch it for a few minutes! How long did those few minutes turn into?).

On the other hand, it could be another excuse. You suddenly realise that your room needs tidying and/or even the ironing becomes a top priority! I am sure that you could add to this rather short list all the things that become more interesting than studying (like cutting the grass!).

The truth is that you are not the only person in the world who feels like that. Most people at one time or another go through it.

What you have to understand is that there are no short cuts or easy ways to study. You need self-discipline and good study skills. But these won't simply come to you; you have to work to acquire them.

How to practise

To help yourself, it is advisable to organise your time. Perhaps you need to make a timetable. In that timetable you put in your study slots, slots for leisure, watching TV, seeing friends and so on. Arrange the timetable in such a way that your study slots do not conflict with your favourite TV programme or when you have to do the ironing! At first it will be difficult, but with time the habit will come and it gets easier.

When you sit down to practise you must focus your mind; you have to concentrate on the task in hand. Therefore, you should plan your week so that you allocate a block of time for practice, about an hour, at least once a week if not more! This should be in addition to the time that you spend studying for the course and doing assignments or projects.

You are allowed one hour to complete each test. You may think that this is more than sufficient time to finish between 30 and 40 questions, but remember that it is not a race. You don't have to be the first person to finish and leave the exam room. If you do complete the test before the hour is up, use the time to check your answers.

When you are practising the tests you should complete the test then double-check your answers before you look at the answers at the back of the book. When you are sure that you have finished – but don't take more than an hour – mark your paper.

Once you have marked your paper look at the questions you got wrong and see if you can spot why. Was it because you misread the question or answer? Was it because you don't know the subject matter? If you are getting more questions wrong in a particular focus area, you need to read up on that.

Dealing with anxiety

It is not uncommon for the majority of people to be anxious prior to taking an exam or test of any kind. It is quite natural to feel tense and nervous when you are put under pressure. Many people worry a lot before taking a test and they also tend to doubt their own ability and begin to think that they are not doing well during the test.

Test anxiety is a common problem for most people. The only difference is the degree to which people worry. Generally, it has been found that a slight amount of anxiety is a good thing, but a large amount is detrimental.

Too much worry and negative thoughts draw attention away from the task in hand, that of taking the test, and thereby disrupt performance. On the other hand, a little anxiety is beneficial; it will help you to be more alert and help your performance.

If you are one of those people who worry too much and have negative thoughts about your performance during a test, you will need to learn to relax. You also need to be more positive. After all, failing a test is not the end of the world though it may seem like it at the time. However, if you practise, this will help to reduce the level of anxiety and therefore should lead to better performance on your part.

The day before the test

One thing you need to do before the actual day of the test (apart from lots of practice!) is to make sure you know exactly where and when the test will be held. There is nothing worse than rushing around trying to find the location of the test centre at the last moment. It is important to arrive at the test centre in good time and to be relaxed, not rushed.

One more thing, do not stay up late or worse, go to a late night rave. The temptation will be there, but fight it!

Things that you are likely to need are:

- a watch (so that you can pace yourself during the test)
- a pencil or two (in case one breaks)
- a pencil sharpener
- an eraser
- a calculator (with its memory erased if it has one)
- a clear head (with memory not erased!)

Do not take any unnecessary items with you to the test. Any bags or books that you have with you in the test room will have to be moved away from your desk, either to the front of the room or to the back.

Make sure you are at the right place at the right time for the right test.

The day of the test

Be at the test room a few minutes before the actual start time so that you can start calming yourself. Remember, you are not the only person who is nervous. All the other people doing the test will be nervous too. It's just that some people show it more than others or, to put it another way, some people are better at hiding it than others!

Once you are in the test room don't worry – at this stage it's too late. In fact, the more you worry the less your mind is able to concentrate on the task in hand – that of doing the test. What you have to do is to go in and do your best.

When the test starts you will not be allowed to talk or make any noise. If you need to ask the invigilator for anything, just put up your hand and wait. If you make too much noise you could be asked (told) to leave the room.

Will I pass?

It is difficult to answer this question. However, if you practise and work hard you will have a much better chance of passing than if you don't. Research has shown that those people who practise and prepare in advance do well compared to those who don't.

With practice you will:

- become more familiar with the format of the test
- become more familiar with the types of question
- become more familiar with the subject matter
- become more self-confident
- be less likely to make mistakes
- be able to identify your strengths as well as weaknesses
- become test wise; and hopefully PASS.

To help you pass you should do the following:

- *Read* the questions carefully, and if you know the answer, mark it on the answer sheet. If you are unsure of the answer, move on to the next question. Don't spend too long on any one question.
- Mark only *one* box on the answer sheet.
- Do not leave any questions *unanswered*. If you do not know the answer, first see if you can eliminate any of the answer choices then make an educated guess. If you leave an answer box blank the answer is WRONG.
- Pace yourself so that you do not run out of *time*. You will have approximately just under two minutes each for most of the questions.
- Read the instructions about how to complete the answer sheet. Make sure you understand what you have to do. Ask if you don't. This is not the time to be shy and timid. Otherwise you could *fail* because of silly mistakes.

Filling in the answer sheet

When you do your test you will be given a test paper, that is the questions and an answer sheet. This answer sheet will have lots of boxes with numbers beside them. The boxes will be labelled with letters A, B, C and D. It is these boxes that you have to fill. The numbers along the side correspond to the question number on the question paper. It is most likely that there will be more boxes on the answer sheet than questions. This is because they are used for many different tests. Some tests have more questions than others.

It is very important to be careful when filling in the answer sheet. It has been known for candidates to fill in the answer box for the wrong question number. For example, say you found question 5 difficult and therefore went on to do question 6, when you come to put your answer on the answer sheet, unless you are careful, you might put the answer for question 6 in the box for question 5.

One other common mistake that candidates make is that when they find questions difficult they move on to the next question, but do not at a later stage come back to those questions and attempt them again, and just leave them unanswered. If you leave any of the questions unanswered you know for certain that you will lose marks.

What you **must** do is to come back to the difficult questions and try to answer them again. If you still cannot work out the answer, you should first eliminate the wrong answers and then make an educated guess. By doing this you are increasing your chances of getting it right. If you leave it blank, you have a 100 per cent chance of getting it **wrong**, but if you are able to eliminate at least two of the choices, you will have at least a 50 per cent chance of getting it **right**.

A 50 per cent chance of getting it right is better than a 100 per cent certainty of getting it wrong!

The answer sheets that you complete are marked by computer. Therefore it is important that you fill in only one answer box, otherwise it will be marked wrong. So if you make a mistake or you wish to change your mind, make sure that you rub out the previous answer.

Some answer sheets have a box which is divided into two. To make a selection you are required to fill in the bottom half of the box. However, if you change your mind and do not want that as your answer, you have to blank out the whole box, ie you then have to fill in the top part of the box as well.

It is important that you read the instructions for completing the answer sheet.

Strategies

A strategy that you could employ is first to mark answers on the question paper and then transfer them to the answer sheet.

If you employ this tactic, do bear in mind that you must leave sufficient time to transfer the answers to the answer sheet. But be careful that you correctly match the question numbers with the numbers on the answer sheet. Also, please ensure that you have not left any question unanswered. Remember, if you do leave a question unanswered, it is definitely the wrong answer!

Another thing that you must remember to do is to make sure that the number of questions corresponds to the number of responses you have made on the answer sheet. *No more and no less.*

Also, do remember to follow the instructions that you are given in the exam, particularly about how to complete the answer sheet. If you are told to make a horizontal mark in the box then do so; don't circle it or put a tick or cross on it!.

Chapter 2
Practice Tests

In this section you will find five practice tests for each of the units that are externally tested. These are:

Unit One   Business Organisations and Employment
Unit Two   People in Business Organisations
Unit Three   Consumers and Customers

The time limit for each paper is one hour.

Before you start the paper it is best to ensure that you will not be disturbed for about an hour. This way you can do the test under timed conditions and therefore be better able to judge your reactions and emotions.

When you have done a test and marked it, make sure you understand why you got the wrong answer for a particular question and are clear about the correct answer before you move on to the next test. *Always make certain that you understand something before you move on.*

Unit One: Business Organisations and Employment
Paper One

Focus One: Purposes and types of business organisations

1   Which of the following would be found in the tertiary sector?

    A   Travel agency   C   Car manufacturer
    B   Zinc mine   D   Oil refinery

2   The BBC is an example of:

    A   a sole trader   C   a public corporation
    B   a plc   D   a private limited
                              company

3   The letters LTD after an organisation's name signify that the company is:

    A   a private limited company   C   a sole trader
    B   a public limited company   D   a partnership

4   Say whether each of the following statements is true or false.

    i)   Public limited liability companies have to send their annual accounts to the exchequer.
    ii) Public limited liability companies must have their annual accounts audited.

    A   True   True   C   False   True
    B   True   False   D   False   False

5   Which of the following will have their shares traded on the Stock Exchange?

    A   a private limited company   C   a public corporation
    B   a public limited company   D   a partnership

6   A public corporation has one of the following characteristics. Which?

    A   privately owned
    B   owned by a large number of shareholders
    C   owned by the government
    D   it is a mutual society without owners

7   The main purpose of a public library is to:

    A   sell books   C   create jobs
    B   provide a public   D   make a profit
        service

8   The main purpose of a partnership business is most likely to be:

    A   to provide a service
    B   to create jobs
    C   to make a profit
    D   to break even over the long term

9   Organisations with a charitable status would normally be found in which sector?

    A   public   C   private
    B   voluntary   D   special

10   The principal objective of an organisation such as British Airways plc is likely to be:

    A   to provide a service
    B   to make a profit
    C   to provide competition
    D   to break even over the long term

11   The principal objective of an organisation such as Oxfam is likely to be:

    A   to make money for its employees
    B   to make a profit
    C   to break even over the long term
    D   to support a special cause

12   Which of the following abbreviations after a company name would signify that it is a private limited company?

    A   PLC   C   LTD
    B   P LIMIT   D   PTD

13 In which of the following business organisations would the owners be personally liable for all the business debts, even when the business is bankrupt?

    A a private limited company
    B a public limited company
    C a public corporation
    D a partnership

Focus two: Business location, environment and products

14 A large supermarket chain is thinking of opening a new store. Which of the following will be its main concern?

    A a large pool of skilled labour
    B a large pool of customers
    C effect of traffic to the environment
    D availability of shop equipment locally

15 Which of the following is a durable product?

    A corn flakes   C body spray
    B washing machine   D cream cake

16 Which of the following is a commercial good?

    A domestic washing machine
    B family car
    C combine harvester
    D domestic microwave oven

17 Which of the following is most likely to be the provider of a public service?

    A BBC   C British Petroleum
    B Ford Motor Company   D Sainsburys

18 A large supermarket chain charges very reasonable prices for its products. What is the main reason for this?

    A legal reasons
    B its concern for poor people
    C competition
    D to keep inflation low

Questions 19 to 21 relate to the following information.

A market research	C sponsorship
B advertising	D after-sales service

Which of the above relate to the following?

19 To find out what consumers think about a new product

    A   B   C   D

20 An arrangement whereby, at a snooker tournament, a company's name and logo are displayed in the arena

    A   B   C   D

21 Sorting out or dealing with problems when customers are unhappy with purchases

    A   B   C   D

22 Which of the following is most likely to be a reason why a company starts a business in an enterprise zone in a deprived region?

A natural resources	C transport services
B government incentives	D labour supply

23 In which of the following categories would a breakfast cereal be found?

A a consumer product	C a durable product
B a commercial product	D a service

24 A factory no longer throws its waste into the local river. Which of the following is the main reason for this?

    A concern for the environment
    B concern for the public
    C concern for the legal implications
    D concern for its competitors

25 Which of the following methods is likely to be most effective in increasing public knowledge about a new product?

    A local sponsorship
    B national advertisements
    C market research
    D improved after-sales service

26   A copper mining company wants to set up in another location.
     Which of the following will be its major concern?

    A   good supply of skilled labour
    B   easy access to customers
    C   good supply of natural resources
    D   existence of a rail service

Focus three: Types of employment

Questions 27 to 29 relate to the following information.

The following are different types of employment:

    A   full-time   C   fixed-term
    B   part-time   D   self-employed

Which of the above best fits the descriptions below?

27   An individual working on his or her own and usually owning
     the business

    A   B   C   D

28   A person who is employed temporarily

    A   B   C   D

29   Over the last ten years or so more women have taken this
     option.

    A   B   C   D

30   Which of the following sectors has seen the most rapid
     increase in terms of employment over the last ten years or
     so?

    A   primary   C   tertiary
    B   secondary   D   manufacturing

Business Organisations and Employment
Paper Two

Focus one: Purposes and types of business organisations

1   Which of the following would not be found in the tertiary sector?

    A   supermarket
    B   further education college
    C   computer manufacturer
    D   building society

2   The main feature of a bureaucratic organisation is:

    A   devolved decision making
    B   a defined hierarchy of authority
    C   equal status for all employees
    D   a flat structure

3   Companies are required by law to pay tax on the profits they make. Which tax would they have to pay?

    A   income tax   C   wealth tax
    B   corporation tax   D   capital gains tax

4   The letters PLC are an abbreviation for

    A   a private limited company
    B   a public limited company
    C   a public listed company
    D   a private listed company

5   What is the primary objective of a local authority funded leisure centre?

    A   profit maximisation   C   to provide a service
    B   to create employment   D   to teach swimming

Questions 6 to 8 share answer options A–D.

An organisation has the following departments:

    A   sales   C   accounts
    B   personnel   D   purchasing

Which of the above departments would be involved in the following activities?

6 Dealing with payment of invoices

    A   B   C   D

7 Acquiring necessary equipment

    A   B   C   D

8 Running an appraisal scheme

    A   B   C   D

9 Which of the following is not solely a provider of a service?

    A teacher   C farmer
    B car washer   D window cleaner

10 Organisations can be in the private or the public sector. Which of the following is in the public sector?

    A British Gas
    B British Broadcasting Corporation
    C British Telecommunications
    D British Airways

11 Bureaucracy within organisations is sometimes referred to as:

    A black tape   C red tape
    B blue tape   D scarlet tape

12 Which of the following is true of a sole trader?

    A limited liability   C shared liability
    B unlimited liability   D no liability

13 A public corporation will be owned by:

    A the government   C the managers
    B the shareholders   D the directors

Focus two: Business location, environment and products

14 Which of the following is a durable product?

    A computer   C fresh milk
    B box of chocolates D frozen chips

15 Which of the following is a commercial good?

    A industrial sewing machine
    B family car
    C domestic microwave oven
    D wrist watch

16   Which of the following is most likely to be a provider of a public service?

    A   IBM   C British Petroleum
    B   Rover Group   D local authority library

Questions 17 to 19 relate to the following information.

There are a number of reasons why businesses locate in certain areas, including the following:

    A   good natural resources   C   government incentives
    B   large pool of labour   D   access to customers

Which of the above reasons is going to be a major factor in the following situations?

17   A business which requires a high degree of manual input

    A   B   C   D

18   The main concern for a retailer

    A   B   C   D

19   A business which is considering locating in a deprived region

    A   B   C   D

20   Which of the following would prompt a business to change its products in line with consumer tastes?

    A   after-sales service   C   Sale of Goods Act
    B   market research   D   product promotion

21   Which of the following would a company use to make consumers more aware of its product nationally?

    A   point of sale display   C   market research
    B   advertising   D   Sale of Goods Act

22   Which of the following is a service?

    A   car paint   C   car engine
    B   car tyre   D   car wash

23   If a company makes consumer goods what type of product is it most likely to be producing?

    A   machine tools   C   industrial tools
    B   DIY tools   D   industrial lathes

24 Which of the following would be used to associate a company or product with a particular sport?

    A   market research   C   capital investment
    B   sponsorship   D   research and
                                      development

25 Many businesses have to pay value added tax. Which of the following would oversee the collection of this?

    A   Inland Revenue
    B   HM Customs and Excise
    C   Department of Social Security
    D   Treasury

26 A company is selling shirts which it claims are pure silk; in fact they are not. Which law is being broken?

    A   Sale of Goods Act
    B   Consumer Protection Act
    C   Health and Safety at Work Act
    D   Trade Descriptions Act

Focus three: Types of employment

27 Which of the following has seen the greatest loss of jobs over the last 20 years?

    A   financial services   C   manufacturing
    B   information technology D   retailing

28 The service sector has been at the forefront of employment creation. Which type of employment has it created the most?

    A   self-employment   C   part-time
    B   full-time   D   job share

29 Which of the following types of work is most likely to be of a temporary nature?

    A   banking   C   fruit picking
    B   education   D   insurance

30 In which type of employment are more women to be found?

    A   full-time   C   fixed-term
    B   part-time   D   self-employed

Business Organisations and Employment
Paper Three

Focus one: Purposes and types of business organisations

1   Which of the following sectors would the NHS be part of?

A   private   C   voluntary
B   public   D   industrial

2   If an organisation is in the primary sector it could be involved in one of the following.

A   making goods
B   mining coal
C   selling ready-made goods
D   providing loans and mortgages

3   A secondary sector product would include all except:

A   a car   C   a computer
B   a car dealer   D   a plain notebook

4   Which of the following sectors would British Gas PLC be part of?

A   private   C   voluntary
B   public   D   industrial

5   Which of the following applies to a charitable organisation?

A   short-term profit maximisation
B   not-for-profit organisation
C   long-term profit maximisation
D   it is insolvent

6   Some organisations' primary objective is to make a profit. There are some whose primary objective is not profit. Which of the following organisations' primary objective is not to make a profit?

A   British Airways   C   British Petroleum
B   British Broadcasting   D   British Gas
    Corporation

7   Which of the following is not in the tertiary sector?

A   solicitor   C   cabinet maker
B   window cleaner   D   plumber

8 Say whether each of the following statements is true (T) or false (F).

i) The programme of privatisation has meant that most of the utilities are now out of the public sector.

ii) As private sector organisations the water companies no longer enjoy the same monopolistic position as when they were in the public sector.

A i) T ii) T   C i) F ii) T
B i) T ii) F   D i) F ii) F

9 A conglomerate can best be described as a business with interests in:

A one activity
B diverse activities
C manufacturing a specific product
D mining for copper

10 In which of the following sectors would you find oil refining?

A primary   C tertiary
B secondary   D voluntary

11 Which of the following most applies to a large private business organisation?

A short-term profit maximisation
B not-for-profit organisation
C long-term profit maximisation
D to become insolvent in the long term

12 A public limited company will be owned by:

A central government   C the local authority
B the shareholders   D the Stock Exchange

13 Which of the following will have unlimited liability?

A Jones and Co Ltd
B Stuart and Sons
C Harry's Ltd
D Feldman PLC

Focus two: Business location, environment and products

14   A large oil exploration company is looking for a new oilfield. Which of the following will be the most important for it in choosing a site?

    A access to customers   C natural resources
    B transport services   D location of other
                                     businesses

15   Which of the following is an example of a service?

    A tv cabinets   C tv repairs
    B tv tubes   D tv cables

16   Which of the following will influence a manufacturer to change its range of products in line with fashion?

    A Sale of Goods Act   C Health and Safety Act
    B public opinion   D consumer rights
                                       legislation

17   Businesses must ensure that products that they sell are of merchantable quality. Which Act places this duty on them?

    A Consumer Protection Act
    B Trade Descriptions Act
    C Sale of Goods Act
    D Health and Safety at Work Act

18   A business supplies office stationery to other businesses. What type of goods is this most likely to be?

    A consumable goods   C industrial goods
    B durable goods   D potential goods

19   A company may use promotion to increase its sales. Which of the following is an example of a promotion?

    A TV commercial   C special offers
    B poster campaign   D radio commercial

20   Say whether each of the following statements is true or false.

    i)   A supplier of car parts is most likely to be located near a vehicle manufacturer.

ii) The government offers money to companies to set up in certain areas.

A	True	True	C	False	True
B	True	False	D	False	False

Questions 21 to 23 relate to the following information.

A	market research	C	promotion
B	advertising	D	after-sales service

Which of the above relate to the following?

21 Finding out what consumers may want in the future

    A   B   C   D

22 Starting a competition in a magazine for teenage girls to win a company's product

    A   B   C   D

23 Commissioning a television commercial

    A   B   C   D

24 Which of the following is a durable product?

A	breakfast cereal	C	gas cooker
B	washing up liquid	D	cream soda

25 Which of the following is a commercial good?

A home washing machine
B industrial lathe
C household vacuum cleaner
D domestic oven

26 Which of the following is most likely to be the provider of a public service?

A	council leisure centre	C	British Gas
B	book shop	D	supermarket

Focus three: Types of employment

27 Which of the following types of employment is most likely to offer better prospects, fringe benefits and working conditions?

A	home-working	C	part-time work
B	temporary work	D	full-time work

28 Which of the following, as providers of jobs, has seen the greatest decline over the last 20 years?

    A shops   C offices

    B factories   D airports

29 The advantage to a company of giving temporary contracts is:

    A an increase in staff motivation

    B an increase in flexibility

    C an increase in salary levels

    D a reduction in fixed costs

30 Which of the following sectors has seen a marked decrease in jobs over the last 10 to 15 years?

    A tertiary sector   C secondary sector

    B service sector   D retail sector

Business Organisations and Employment
Paper Four

Focus one: Purposes and types of business organisation

1 Organisations such as travel agencies and hotels would be part of which sector?

   A primary   C tertiary
   B secondary   D leisure

2 Say whether each of the following statements is true (T) or false (F).

   i)   A garage repairing cars would be found in the tertiary sector.

   ii) An insurance sales representative would be found in the tertiary sector.

   A i) T   ii) T   C i) F   ii) T
   B i) T   ii) F   D i) F   ii) F

3 Which of the following will have its shares traded on the Stock Exchange?

   A a private limited company
   B a public limited company
   C a public corporation
   D a partnership

4 Say whether each of the following statements is true or false.

   i)   An organisation registered as a charity has an obligation to make a profit for its trustees.

   ii) Charitable organisations have an obligation to minimise their costs.

   A True   True   C False   True
   B True   False   D False   False

5 Public limited companies are required by law to hold an AGM. What is an AGM?

   A A Grand Meeting
   B Annual General Meeting
   C Annual Give-away Meeting (dividends)
   D A Great Meeting

6 Some organisations are not-for-profit organisations. Which of the following falls within that category?

    A private limited company
    B public limited company
    C partnerships
    D company limited by guarantee

7 Which of the following is an example of a private sector business?

    A British Broadcasting Corporation
    B a local authority gym
    C British Nuclear Fuels
    D a bank

8 Which of the following has limited liability?

    A J Smith, grocer   C Word Tech Ltd
    B H Shah and Partners   D A S Crooke and Son

9 A coal mining company would be part of which sector?

    A primary   C tertiary
    B secondary   D leisure

10 The main aim of a sole trader's local newsagents shop will be to:

    A create jobs
    B provide income for the owner
    C provide a public service
    D provide profit for shareholders

11 In which of the following sectors would you find farming?

    A primary   C tertiary
    B secondary   D voluntary

12 In which of the following sectors does the Ford Motor Company mainly operate?

    A primary   C tertiary
    B secondary   D voluntary

13 The main aim of a local authority funded library will be to

    A create jobs
    B provide income for the owner
    C provide a public service
    D provide profit for shareholders

Focus two: Business location, environment and products

14 A business supplies dairy products to other retailers. What type of goods are these most likely to be?

    A consumable goods   C industrial goods
    B durable goods   D potential goods

15 A company making fashion jewellery for export to Europe wants to relocate to another town in England. Which of the following will be the most important for them in choosing a site?

    A access to customers   C natural resources
    B transport services   D location of other
                                           businesses

16 Which of the following is an example of a consumable product?

    A washing machine   C microcomputer
    B shaving cream   D freezer

17 A household dishwasher would be in which category?

    A commercial product   C consumer durable
    B consumable product   product
                                     D industrial product

Questions 18 to 20 relate to the following.

There are a number of reasons why a business chooses to locate in a certain area, including:

    A access to customers
    B access to government grants
    C access to business customers
    D access to a pool of workers

Which of the above would apply to the following?

18 A manufacturer wants non-repayable finance

    A   B   C   D

19 A company uses labour-intensive manufacturing methods

    A   B   C   D

20 A company makes parts for other manufacturers' products

    A   B   C   D

Questions 21 to 23 relate to the following.

    A   Inland Revenue
    B   HM Customs and Excise
    C   Health and Safety Executive
    D   Department of Social Security

Which of the above relate to the following?

21   Collecting corporation tax

    A   B   C   D

22   Collecting national insurance contributions

    A   B   C   D

23   Collecting value added tax

    A   B   C   D

24   A company is attempting to sell computers which it claims are made in Britain, when in fact they have been imported from abroad. Which legislation would stop them claiming this?

    A   Health and Safety at Work Act
    B   Trade Descriptions Act
    C   Sale of Goods Act
    D   Consumer Protection Act

25   A company is offering free samples of a new shampoo. Which of the following activities is it undertaking?

    A   market research   C   promotion
    B   advertising   D   after-sales service

26   The same company then wants to find out what people think about the shampoo. Which activity will it undertake?

    A   promotion   C   market research
    B   after-sales service   D   advertising

Focus three: Types of employment

Questions 27 to 29 relate to the following information.

The following are different types of employment:

A   full-time   C   fixed-term
B   part-time   D   self-employed

Which of the above best fits the descriptions below?

27   A freelance consultant is quite likely to take this option

   A   B   C   D

28   A person who is on a short-term contract

   A   B   C   D

29   Many students take this option when studying full time

   A   B   C   D

30   Many companies hire staff at busy periods during the year.
     Which type of contract is most likely to be offered?

   A   permanent   C   job share
   B   temporary   D   flexible

Business Organisations and Employment
Paper Five

Focus one: Purposes and types of business organisations

1   Decide whether each of the following statements is true (T) or false (F).

  i)   An optician is part of the secondary sector.

  ii) A self-employed motor mechanic is part of the tertiary sector.

A	(i) T	(ii) T		C	(i) F	(ii) T
B	(i) T	(ii) F		D	(i) F	(ii) F

2   Organisations such as Disneyland and hotels would be found in which sector?

A	primary	C	tertiary
B	secondary	D	mining

3   An organisation which is involved in all three sectors – primary, secondary and tertiary – is said to be integrated. Which way?

A	horizontally	C	laterally
B	vertically	D	adversely

4   A public sector company will be owned by:

A	the government	C	the managers
B	the shareholders	D	the Stock Exchange

5   Say whether each of the following statements is true (T) or false (F).

  i)   Organisations cannot be registered as a charity if their prime motive is profit maximisation.

  ii) A company limited by guarantee will not have the making of a profit as its primary goal.

A	i) T	ii) T		C	i) F	ii) T
B	i) T	ii) F		D	i) F	ii) F

6   What tax would a sole trader be liable to pay on profit earned?

A	corporation tax	C	income tax
B	capital transfer tax	D	value added tax

7   Which of the following types of business is most likely to be set up as a partnership?

    A   firm of accountants   C   supermarket
    B   newsagents shop   D   distribution company

8   Which of the following is a legal entity in its own right?

    A   J Smith, grocer   C   Word Tech Ltd
    B   H Shah and Partners   D   A S Crooke and Son

9   Which of the following is to be found in the voluntary sector?

    A   a limited company
    B   a public limited company
    C   a company limited by guarantee
    D   a partnership

10   Which of the following businesses can sell its shares on the stock market?

    A   Ultra High Tech Ltd
    B   Technologies Plc
    C   A S Brooke and Daughter
    D   P M Partnership

11   Which of the following will be required to pay income tax?

    A   Word Tech Ltd   C   Technologies Plc
    B   A S Crooke and Son   D   M M & M Ltd

12   A public sector organisation's profits will go to:

    A   the shareholders   C   the Stock Exchange
    B   the government   D   the managers

13   Which sector of the economy has seen the most growth in recent years?

    A   primary   C   tertiary
    B   secondary   D   manufacturing

Focus two: Business location, environment and products

14   A company wants to set up a plant to make cement, which requires chalk. Which of the following will most influence its choice for the location of the new plant?

    A   labour supply
    B   natural resources
    C   proximity of other businesses
    D   government grants

15   A company may use promotion to increase its sales. Which of the following is an example of a promotion?

    A   cinema advertisements
    B   free samples
    C   magazine advertisements
    D   radio commercial

Questions 16 to 18 relate to the following.

    A   Sale of Goods Act
    B   Consumer Protection Act
    C   Health and Safety at Work Act
    D   Trade Descriptions Act

The above are laws which aim to protect consumers. Which of the above Acts would be used in the following situations?

16   A company does not sell goods of merchantable quality.

    A   B   C   D

17   A company claims that a gold bracelet is solid 22 carats, when they know that it is only 9 carat gold.

    A   B   C   D

18   A company advertises a product for £25 cash without saying that VAT would be added.

    A   B   C   D

19   A high tech company is locating a new plant in an inner city deprived area. Which of the following is most likely to be the reason for this decision?

    A   natural resources
    B   large pool of unskilled labour
    C   a government grant for start-up costs
    D   good transport links

20   A company gets a famous tennis player to use its rackets at tournaments, in return for free rackets and a fee. Which activity is the company undertaking?

    A   advertising   C   promotion
    B   sponsorship   D   after-sales service

21   Which of the following products would be aimed specifically at large businesses?

    A   personal computers   C   domestic fridges
    B   mainframe computers   D   laptop computers

22   Which of the following could a company use to promote its products and gain market share?

    A   market research   C   capital investment
    B   sponsorship   D   research and
                              development

23   To gain market share a company offers customers two products for the price of one. Which technique is it using?

    A   advertisement   C   product development
    B   promotion   D   market research

24   A company used to sell fur coats but stopped selling them because of widespread disapproval. Which of the following is likely to have had the most influence?

    A   shortage of fur
    B   public opinion
    C   concern for the environment
    D   too much competition

25   Which of the following is a consumable good?

    A   photocopying paper   C   photocopier
    B   laser printer   D   personal computer

26   Mr Singh is thinking of opening a small corner shop selling groceries. Which of the following factors will he consider the most important?

    A   a pool of labour
    B   availability of customers
    C   car parking facilities
    D   good transport services

Focus three: Types of employment

27   Which of the following types of work is most likely to be of a temporary nature?

    A   banking   C   teaching in schools
    B   harvesting vegetables   D   nursing

28   The most dramatic fall in employment has been in one of the following. Which?

    A   retailing   C   mining
    B   financial services   D   leisure services

29   The hotel industry is most likely to take on extra staff during which period?

    A   January – March   C   June – August
    B   April – May   D   September – November

30   Someone who needs to work but has nursery age children is most likely to opt for one of the following types of employment. Which?

    A   full-time permanent
    B   part-time permanent
    C   full-time temporary
    D   full-time self-employment

Unit Two: People in Business Organisations
Paper One

Focus one: Organisational structures and working arrangements

1   Say whether each of the following statements is true or false.

i)   Organisations with a hierarchical structure tend to have long lines of communication between the lower levels and top management.

ii)   The Civil Service is an example of an organisation with a hierarchical structure.

A   True   True   C   False   True
B   True   False   D   False   False

2   An organisation with a flat structure is characterised by one of the following:

A   many levels of authority
B   few levels of authority
C   long lines of communication
D   highly centralised systems

3   An organisation with many levels of authority is termed what?

A   historical   C   horizontal
B   hierarchical   D   humanistic

4   An organisation chart would show which of the following?

A   names of post holders
B   lines of communication
C   salary ranges
D   annual leave arrangements

5   Where the head office of an organisation carries out the administration, what type of structure is it most likely to be?

A   centralised   C   commercialised
B   decentralised   D   matrix

6   Which of the following departments is most likely to be concerned with making goods?

A   purchasing   C   accounting
B   human resources   D   production

Questions 7 to 9 relate to the following information.

    A   personnel
    B   distribution
    C   research and development
    D   marketing

Which of the above departments would be responsible for the following?

7   Identifying potential customers

    A   B   C   D

8   Recruiting and selecting employees

    A   B   C   D

9   Organising deliveries

    A   B   C   D

10 An employee works during the day one week and during the night the following week on a continuous basis. What type of arrangement is this?

    A   flexi-time   C   shift work
    B   temporary work   D   centralised work

11 Which of the following departments is most likely to be concerned with issuing invoices?

    A   purchasing   C   accounting
    B   human resources D   production

12 In which of the following would two people be employed to do the same job at different times and the salary be divided between them?

    A   flexi-time   C   part-time
    B   job share   D   centralised work

Focus two: Employee and employer rights and responsibilities

13 If a non-union employee is called to a disciplinary hearing he or she has the right to be accompanied by:

    A   their manager
    B   a trade union representative
    C   a person of their choice
    D   nobody

14 Which of the following is a method of consultation?

  A   redundancy announcement
  B   regular meetings
  C   a directive
  D   a notice to inform of changes

15 Firms have a legal duty to carry out the provisions of the Race Relations Act. These are to stop discrimination on the grounds of all except:

  A   skin colour   C   creed
  B   ethnic origin   D   gender

16 Say whether each of the following statements is true (T) or false (F).

  i)   The current employment legislation states that a contract of employment must be issued to a new employee within three months of starting work.

  ii) Where an employee has been employed part-time for at least one year then that employee would be able to claim redundancy payments in the event of being made redundant.

  A   i) T   ii) T   C   i) F   ii) T
  B   i) T   ii) F   D   i) F   ii) F

17 Which of the following would not form a part of the contract of employment?

  A   period of notice   C   holiday entitlement
  B   frequency of payments   D   marital status

18 Say whether each of the following statements is true (T) or false (F).

  i)   The contract of employment which is signed by both the employer and employee is not a legally binding document, as disputes are only dealt with by an industrial tribunal.

  ii) The health and safety law places total responsibility on the employee in the work place.

  A   i) T   ii) T   C   i) F   ii) T
  B   i) T   ii) F   D   i) F   ii) F

19   Say whether each of the following statements is true (T) or false (F).

   i)   Some organisations require all their employees to belong to a single trade union. They can therefore refuse employment to those unwilling to join a union.

   ii)   It would be fair to dismiss an employee for joining a trade union different from the one that the majority of the workers belonged to.

   A   i) T   ii) T   C   i) F   ii) T
   B   i) T   ii) F   D   i) F   ii) F

20   Employees have a contractual and a moral duty to:

   A   be pleasant to colleagues
   B   have high integrity
   C   set a good example
   D   refrain from delegating work

21   Employees can choose to be part of a collective bargaining process. Which parties would normally be involved?

   A   CBI and TUC
   B   union reps and employers
   C   union reps and members
   D   unions reps and government

22   Firms have a legal duty to carry out the provisions of the Sex Discrimination Act. These are to stop discrimination on the grounds of all except:

   A   sexual orientation   C   creed
   B   marital status   D   gender

23   Employers and employees have certain expectations from each other. Which of the following would an employer find *not* acceptable?

   A   not to discriminate   C   not to be abusive
   B   not to be honest   D   not be disobedient

24   Below are reasons why an employer may dismiss an employee. Which one would be unfair?

   A   sexual harassment   C   joining a union
   B   racial harassment   D   physical violence

Focus three: Job roles within business organisations

25 A managing director will mainly be concerned with which of the following?

> A   implementing policy decisions
> B   formulating policies
> C   day-to-day running of the company
> D   hiring and firing of workers

26 In most large organisations strategic policy decisions would be taken by:

> A   board of directors
> B   director of personnel
> C   director of production
> D   trade union representative

27 Beds Ltd is a company making beds. Whose responsibility will it be to look after the shop-floor work?

> A   an operative   C   a manager
> B   a supervisor   D   a director

28 In an organisation who would be responsible for success or failure?

> A   production supervisor   C   finance director
> B   manager   D   managing director

29 The staff working in the personnel department of an organisation would deal with all the following except:

> A   issuing contracts
> B   staff welfare
> C   product development
> D   recruitment and selection

30 A press release would normally be issued by someone working in one of the following departments. Which?

> A   personnel   C   public relations
> B   accounts   D   customer services

People in Business Organisations
Paper Two

Focus one: Organisational structures and working arrangements

1 Say whether each of the following statements is true or false.

i) The way in which an organisation structures itself is affected by its size, in terms of number of employees.

ii) The mission statement is a corporate takeover plan written by the directors of the company.

A	True	True	C	False	True
B	True	False	D	False	False

2 Which of the following best describes a hierarchical organisation?

    A a broad span of control
    B clear chain of command
    C few levels of authority
    D autonomous project teams

3 The main feature of a decentralised organisation is

    A devolved decision making
    B a defined hierarchy of authority
    C equal status for all employees
    D a flat structure

4 James and Susan work for a large publishing company and do the same job. James works in the afternoons and Susan works in the mornings. This type of arrangement is called what?

A	flexi-time	C	fixed term
B	part time	D	job sharing

Questions 5 to 7 relate to the following information.

A	personnel	C	research and
B	distribution		development
		D	marketing

Which of the above departments would be responsible for the following?

5   Finding out what customers want

     A   B   C   D

6   Dealing with employees' welfare issues

     A   B   C   D

7   Looking at possibilities for future products

     A   B   C   D

Questions 8 to 10 relate to the following.

A	centralised	C	flat
B	matrix	D	hierarchical

Which of the following relate to the above?

8   The decision making is done at head office.

     A   B   C   D

9   There are many levels of authority.

     A   B   C   D

10   There are only a few levels of authority.

     A   B   C   D

11   Which department has the responsibility for finding out what customers want?

A	research and development	C	marketing
B	sales	D	production

12   Which department has the responsibility for buying the resources that the company needs?

A	marketing	C	purchasing
B	production	D	accounting

Focus two: Employee and employer rights and responsibilities

13   An employee has both a legal and an ethical duty not to:

A	delegate work	C	set a good example
B	be racist	D	be honest

Questions 14 to 16 share answer options A to D.

A   comply with health and safety legislation
B   comply with race relations legislation
C   comply with employer's rules and regulations
D   comply with sex discrimination legislation

Which of the above relate to the following situations?

14   An employee refuses to wear goggles when doing welding work.

A   B   C   D

15   An employee refuses to work with female colleagues.

A   B   C   D

16   A number of employees are tormenting a colleague for wearing a turban.

A   B   C   D

17   An employee believes that she has been unfairly dismissed. What action is most likely?

A   go to court
B   go to ACAS
C   go to an industrial tribunal
D   go and picket at the gates

18   An employer would be well within his rights to sack an employee without warning for one of the following reasons. Which?

A   joining a trade union
B   becoming a shop steward
C   being late
D   gross misconduct

19   All employees are required to take reasonable care when working and must not endanger their colleagues. What legislation places this duty on the employee?

A   Employment Protection Act
B   Health and Safety at Work Act
C   Race Relations Act
D   Data Protection Act

20   Say whether each of the following statements is true (T) or false (F).

i)   All contracts and other terms and conditions of employment have to be negotiated by union representatives.

ii)   An employee attending a disciplinary hearing can take along a friend.

A   i) T   ii) T   C   i) F   ii) T
B   i) T   ii) F   D   i) F   ii) F

21   Say whether each of the following statements is true (T) or false (F).

i)   Where an employer recognises a trade union all new recruits are required to join that union.

ii)   It would be unfair to dismiss an employee for joining a trade union.

A   i) T   ii) T   C   i) F   ii) T
B   i) T   ii) F   D   i) F   ii) F

22   A trade union is there for the benefit of:

A   employer   C   shareholders
B   members   D   clients of the firm

23   The management of a company recognise the importance of employee co-operation and participation in running the firm. Which of the following is most likely to involve staff members?

A   issuing a statement of intent
B   circulating management decisions
C   team meetings
D   a management directive

24   Say whether each of the following statements is true or false.

i)   An employee gets drunk during working hours and causes damage in the work place. The employer can sack him instantly.

ii)   An employee is guilty of sexual harassment. The employee can be sacked instantly.

A   True   True   C   False   True
B   True   False   D   False   False

Focus three: Job roles within business organisations

25 Say whether each of the following statements is true (T) or false (F).

i)   A company secretary's role would include dealing with shareholders' correspondence.

ii) A company secretary's role would also include taking minutes at team meetings.

A i) T   ii) T   C i) F   ii) T
B i) T   ii) F   D i) F   ii) F

26 The employees working within the accounts department of an organisation would deal with all of the following except:

A   monitoring budgets   C   sending invoices
B   payroll   D   product promotion

27 The chief executive of a large business organisation would on the whole be concerned with which of the following levels of business operation?

A   day-to-day activities   C   long-term decisions
B   weekly payroll   D   shop-floor activities

28 Which of the following would deal with clerical errors to do with wages?

A   sales clerk   C   personnel assistant
B   payroll clerk   D   MD's secretary

29 One of the responsibilities of managers is to:

A   decide on strategic polices
B   implement organisational policies
C   check all letters sent out
D   check all incoming mail

30 A person writing delivery schedules would be involved with which activity?

A   security   C   selling
B   distribution   D   production

People in Business Organisations
Paper Three

Focus one: Organisational structures and working arrangements

1   A company has decided to alter the way in which its employees currently work. They have decided to set up project teams. They have done this because:

    A   it gives management more control
    B   employees can keep a check on each other
    C   it can increase the productivity of employees
    D   it may give job security

Questions 2 to 4 relate to the departments of a company.

    A   marketing   C   computer services
    B   sales   D   customer services

Which of the above departments would be responsible for the following?

2   Getting orders for the products that the company makes

    A   B   C   D

3   Making sure that the company produces goods that meet customer needs

    A   B   C   D

4   Maintaining company's databases

    A   B   C   D

5   Which department would be responsible for providing the clerical support?

    A   human resources   C   customer services
    B   administration   D   distribution

6   How would you describe an organisation in which decisions have to be passed down through many levels before they can be implemented?

    A   centralised   C   hierarchical
    B   flat   D   matrix

7   A company decides to set up a new team to check all products before they are sent out. What is the aim of this?

    A   to increase productivity
    B   to increase quality control

    C   to increase competition
    D   to increase jobs

8   A security company operates 24 hours a day. The security guards work for 12 hours at a time. What type of working arrangement is this?

    A   flexi-hours
    B   fixed term

    C   shifts
    D   decentralised

Questions 9 to 11 relate to the following working arrangements.

    A   permanent
    B   fixed term

    C   centralised
    D   flexible

Which of the above applies to the following situations?

9   A supermarket hires extra staff for the Christmas period.

    A   B   C   D

10   All purchases are made by the head office.

    A   B   C   D

11   Employees can start and finish work at different times of the day.

    A   B   C   D

12   An organisation in which employees are responsible to more than one line manager would be described as:

    A   centralised
    B   flat

    C   hierarchical
    D   matrix

Focus two: Employee and employer rights and responsibilities

13   Say whether each of the following statements is true (T) or false (F).

i)   An employer cannot be held liable for discrimination by an employee.

ii)   An employer will be held liable for direct discrimination.

A i) T   ii) T   C i) F   ii) T
B i) T   ii) F   D i) F   ii) F

14 An employee has both a legal and an ethical duty not to:

A be on time   C set a good example
B be obedient   D discriminate

Questions 15 to 17 relate to the following information.

Employees have rights and responsibilities. The following are responsibilities.

A work towards company's objectives
B comply with terms of contract
C refrain from discriminating
D meet customer needs

Which of the above responsibilities relate to the following situations?

15 A small number of employees go on an unofficial strike.

A   B   C   D

16 An employee's carelessness has resulted in increased wastage.

A   B   C   D

17 A worker refuses to cooperate with other workers from a minority ethnic background.

A   B   C   D

18 A large company which employs 500 people is required by law to have a certain type of insurance. What type of insurance must it have?

A national insurance
B employers' liability insurance
C employees' liability insurance
D life insurance for all employees

19 Which of the following is a legal responsibility of the employer with reference to health and safety?

A to provide first aid training for all staff
B to provide weekly training on health and safety
C to record all accidents in a book
D to test fire alarms each day

20 An employee has been warned on two occasions about his behaviour at work. Which of the following will the employer use if his behaviour does not improve?

    A grievance procedure
    B professional development
    C disciplinary procedure
    D negotiate conditions of service

21 Many large employers tend to provide training for their staff. What is the reason for this?

    A to increase staff turnover
    B to decrease staff turnover
    C to improve relations with staff
    D to provide appropriate skills

22 An employee has been ridiculed by a manager in front of other people. The employee feels humiliated. What is the most appropriate action to take in this situation?

    A sue the manager in a court of law
    B use the grievance procedure
    C try to humiliate the manager
    D use physical violence

23 All employers are obliged to issue a contract or a statement of terms and conditions of employment. Which of the following would not form a part of the contract of employment?

    A hours of work   C named line manager
    B frequency of payments D holiday entitlement

24 If an employee thinks that she has been unfairly dismissed which body should she take her case to?

    A industrial tribunal
    B the House of Lords
    C the criminal court
    D the European Court of Human Rights

Focus three: Job roles within business organisations

25 Which of the following would a board of directors be most concerned with?

    A day-to-day functioning of the company
    B the grievances currently outstanding
    C strategic planning
    D the production targets for the next two months

26 A production operative is someone who is:

    A in charge of production targets
    B responsible for making goods
    C in charge of the department
    D responsible for supervising

27 A supervisor of a large manufacturing company would on the whole be concerned with which of the following levels of business operation?

    A operational
    B tactical
    C strategic
    D making policy decisions

Questions 28 to 30 relate to the following functions.

    A security   C distributing
    B cleaning   D producing

    Which of the above apply to the following?

28 Ensuring that theft is minimised

    A   B   C   D

29 Ensuring that delivery targets are met

    A   B   C   D

30 Ensuring that goods are made

    A   B   C   D

People in Business Organisations
Paper Four

Focus one: Organisational structures and working arrangements

Questions 1 to 3 relate to the following.

A	fixed-term contracts	C	flexi-time
B	permanent contracts	D	shift work

Which of the above apply to the following circumstances?

1   Where employees need to be able to start and finish work at different times

     A   B   C   D

2   Where the company operates 24 hours a day and groups of employees work at different times of the day for fixed periods

     A   B   C   D

3   Where an employer needs someone for a limited period

     A   B   C   D

4   Which of the following departments is most likely to set up and run an induction programme for new recruits?

A	finance	C	customer services
B	administration	D	personnel

Questions 5 to 7 relate to the following.

A   research and development
B   distribution
C   customer services
D   production

Which of the above departments would be responsible in the following situations?

5   Ensuring a high level of client satisfaction

     A   B   C   D

6   Ensuring that manufacturing targets are met

     A   B   C   D

7   Generating and testing new ideas

     A   B   C   D

8   A pyramid organisation is one which is:

     A   flat   C   matrix
     B   hierarchical   D   ancient

9   An organisation in which a member of staff may report to more than one line manager is referred to as what?

     A   flat   C   matrix
     B   hierarchical   D   ancient

10 A fireworks company takes on temporary workers in September for about two months. What is the main purpose of this?

     A   to give holidays to permanent staff
     B   to increase productivity
     C   to become more competitive
     D   to increase automation

11 A production operative is most likely to be:

     A   based in an office   C   based in a shop
     B   based in a factory   D   mobile

12 An accounts clerk is most likely to be:

     A   based in an office   C   based in a shop
     B   based in a factory   D   mobile

Focus two: Employee and employer rights and responsibilities

13 An employee has both a legal and a moral duty not to:

     A   be honest   C   set a good example
     B   delegate work   D   be abusive

14 Current employment law requires that an employer, within a specified period, issue a new recruit with :

     A   company rulebook
     B   health and safety policy
     C   terms and conditions of work
     D   equal opportunity policy

Questions 15 to 17 relate to the following information.

Employees have rights and responsibilities. The following are rights.

    A   to be paid on time
    B   to belong to a trade union
    C   to have a lunch break
    D   to have appropriate safety equipment

Which rights have not been met in the following situations?

15 The introduction of new drilling machines without hand guards

    A   B   C   D

16 A refusal to allow time for refreshments

    A   B   C   D

17 An unreasonable delay in receiving remuneration

    A   B   C   D

18 The increased use of consultation between employer and employees can be beneficial. The employees are more likely to feel:

    A equal   C motivated
    B skilled   D threatened

19 An employee is likely to seek the assistance of his union representative in which of the following situations?

    A   to get a reference for another job
    B   to get a testimonial
    C   attending a disciplinary hearing
    D   to get extra overtime

20 The primary purpose of a staff association can be described as:

    A   to negotiate with trade unions
    B   to deal with industrial relations
    C   to arrange staff training
    D   to arrange health and safety inspections

21 Say whether each of the following statements is true or false.

    i)   A trade union will negotiate with management on behalf of members on how best to increase productivity without increased costs.

    ii)   A trade union official is not allowed to represent a member at a disciplinary hearing.

    A True True   C False True
    B True False   D False False

Questions 22 to 24 relate to the following information.

A company is considering ways in which employees could be encouraged to become more cooperative and to take an interest in the performance of the company. The following are some of the methods.

    A   introduce a share ownership scheme
    B   set up quality circles
    C   offer job security
    D   set up a bonus scheme

Which of the above could help in the following situations?

22 To reduce anxiety about possible redundancies

    A   B   C   D

23 To take pride in their work

    A   B   C   D

24 To meet production targets at certain times of the year

    A   B   C   D

Focus three: Job roles within business organisations

25 A company secretary's role would include one of the following:

    A   take minutes at departmental meetings
    B   deal with shareholders' correspondence
    C   book meetings for a departmental manager
    D   type letters for a departmental manager

Questions 26 to 28 relate to the following information.

Listed below are different job roles within a retail organisation:

A   sales assistant   C   manager
B   supervisor   D   area manager

Which of the above would carry out the following?

26   Be available on the shop floor at most times of the day to serve patrons

A   B   C   D

27   Have overall responsibility for the smooth running of the emporium

A   B   C   D

28   Be responsible for stores in a certain geographical location

A   B   C   D

29   Which of the following staff would be responsible for the day-to-day running of a department?

A   director
B   manager
C   oldest person in department
D   supervisor

30   The ultimate responsibility for the success or failure of a company will rest with the:

A   departmental manager   C   personnel director
B   chief executive   D   finance director

People in Business Organisations
Paper Five

Focus one: Organisational structures and working arrangements

1   Identify the most correct description of a hierarchical organisation.

   A   long lines of communication and many levels of authority
   B   short lines of communication and few levels of authority
   C   short lines of communication and many levels of authority
   D   long lines of communication and few levels of authority

2   Identify the most correct description of a flat organisation.

   A   long lines of communication and many levels of authority
   B   short lines of communication and few levels of authority
   C   short lines of communication and many levels of authority
   D   long lines of communication and few levels of authority

Questions 3 to 5 relate to the following departments.

   A   production   C   accounting
   B   purchasing   D   computer services

Which of the above departments would be responsible for the following?

3   Maintaining the company's software

   A   B   C   D

4   Controlling what is made and when

   A   B   C   D

5   Making financial forecasts

   A   B   C   D

6   Which department would be responsible for the recruitment
    and selection process?

    A   human resources   C   customer services
    B   administration   D   distribution

7   A police station operates 24 hours a day, with teams of officers
    working 8 hours at a time on a rota basis. What is this type of
    arrangement called?

    A   flexi-hours   C   fixed term
    B   shift working   D   job sharing

8   Which of the following departments would be responsible
    for drawing up job descriptions and issuing terms and
    conditions of employment?

    A   accounts   C   administration
    B   research and   D   human resources
          development

9   An organisation employs students during the summer
    holidays on a temporary basis. What type of contract would
    the students be given?

    A   permanent   C   flexible
    B   fixed term   D   students do not need
                            one

Questions 10 and 11 relate to the following.

A computer manufacturer has teams of workers assembling
computers.

10   Each team which exceeds its target is paid a bonus. Why does
     the company do this?

    A   to improve quality assurance
    B   to improve productivity
    C   to improve working conditions
    D   to improve earnings of workers

11   The bonus is reduced if any computers are found to be faulty
     when tested. Why does the company do this?

    A   to improve quality assurance
    B   to improve productivity
    C   to improve working conditions
    D   to improve job security

12   Rhea works full time but she prefers to start work late. She then makes up the hours by finishing late. She can do this because the company allows:

    A   job sharing   C   part-time work
    B   flexi-time   D   overtime

Focus two: Employee and employer rights and responsibilities

13   A medium-sized organisation has decided to train a majority of its staff so that they become multi-skilled. What is the reasoning behind this?

    A   to improve industrial relations
    B   to improve staff consultation
    C   to offer job security
    D   to improve staff productivity

14   An employee has worked for a manufacturing firm for ten years as a manual worker. The manager of the firm tells the employee on a Friday that he is now redundant and should not turn up for work on Monday morning. Which body is most likely to deal with this case?

    A   a staff association
    B   Equal Opportunities Commission
    C   industrial tribunal
    D   European Court of Human Rights

15   The primary purpose of a trade union is to protect the interests of:

    A   parliamentary members
    B   council members
    C   political party members
    D   paid-up members

Questions 16 to 18 relate to the following information.

The use of the following can improve industrial relations and increase motivational levels in employees.

A	bonus scheme	C	social amenities
B	share scheme	D	job security

Which of the above could be used for the following?

16 Make employees feel they have a stake in the company

    A   B   C   D

17 Encourage workers to mix out of work time

    A   B   C   D

18 Encourage workers to work harder at particular points in time

    A   B   C   D

19 Whose responsibility is health and safety in an organisation?

    A   Health and Safety Executive
    B   employers and employees
    C   local authority inspectors
    D   employees of the company

20 Say whether each of the following statements is true or false.

i)   An employee may be asked to carry out any reasonable duty even though it is not listed in the contract of employment.

ii)   An employee can be sued for revealing confidential information about his company.

A	True	True	C	False True
B	True	False	D	False False

21 An employee must have worked for a certain number of years for a company before becoming eligible for redundancy payments. How many years?

A	5 years	C	3 years
B	4 years	D	2 years

22 All employers are obliged to issue a contract or a statement of terms and conditions of employment. Which of the following would not form a part of the contract of employment?

    A hours of work
    B frequency of payments
    C redundancy pay details
    D holiday entitlement

23 A company decides to change the terms and conditions of work. What is the best way forward to gain the cooperation of staff?

    A inform each worker by letter of the change
    B arrange a meeting of all workers and tell them of the change
    C meet with worker representatives to discuss the change
    D issue a directive of the changes that will take place

24 A company decides to survey its workforce about job satisfaction. It wants to increase job satisfaction if possible. Why?

    A to increase stress levels   C to decrease wages
    B to increase staff   D to decrease absenteeism
       turnover

Focus three: Job roles within business organisations

25 Which of the following would a production manager be most concerned with?

    A day-to-day functioning of the company
    B the grievances currently outstanding
    C strategic planning
    D the production targets for the next two months

26 A company sells its products through retailers. Which department will be responsible for persuading retailers to stock its products?

    A marketing   C sales
    B production   D accounts

Questions 27 to 29 relate to the following information.

Listed below are different job roles within an organisation.

A   distribution manager
B   finance manager
C   administration manager
D   personnel manager

Which of the above would have responsibility for the following?

27   Ensuring that the redundancy paper work is appropriately completed

A   B   C   D

28   Ensuring that delivery schedules minimise time wastage

A   B   C   D

29   Monitoring cash flow to ensure that bank overdraft is used minimally

A   B   C   D

30   Which department would be responsible for finding out what consumers want?

A   marketing   C   sales
B   production   D   accounts

Unit Three: Consumers and Customers
Paper One

Focus one: Importance of consumers and customers

The following can cause changes in demand for goods and services.

      A   increase in cost of living
      B   confidence to spend
      C   advertising
      D   changing wants

Which of the above applies to the following?

1   People spending more on basic goods and less on luxuries

      A   B   C   D

2   An increase in the demand for consumer durables

      A   B   C   D

3   Keeping in line with fashionable trends

      A   B   C   D

4   An insurance company wants to launch a new pension plan. Which of the following characteristics is the company most likely to be interested in?

      A   tastes   C   age
      B   gender   D   ethnicity

5   A local primary school is undertaking some research to find out the potential demand for its services over the next year. Which characteristic would it be investigating?

      A   tastes   C   age
      B   gender   D   ethnicity

6   A supermarket offers its customers 'points' when they shop there. The number of points offered depends on the amount spent. The points can then be converted to money and used for shopping. Why does it offer this?

      A   to encourage repeat business
      B   to ensure the survival of the business
      C   as a source of information to customers
      D   to reduce the level of income from each sale

7   Say whether each of the following statements is true or false.

i)   Disposable income is the money that people have before tax is deducted.

ii)   Disposable income can be a measure of a person's spending power.

A   True   True   C   False   True
B   True   False   D   False   False

Questions 8 to 10 relate to the following trends.

A   increased sales of non-alcoholic lagers
B   increased sales of foreign holidays
C   increase in the number of DIY superstores
D   increase in the number of out-of-town supermarkets

Which of the above relates to the following?

8   More people choose to travel abroad nowadays

A   B   C   D

9   Drink-drivers face heavy penalties

A   B   C   D

10   More people are choosing to carry out home improvements by themselves

A   B   C   D

11   Demand is most likely to increase if one of the following happens.

A   increase in unemployment
B   increase in interest rates
C   decrease in unemployment
D   decrease in disposable income

Focus two: Types of promotion in business

12   A shop has a display at the checkout. What type of promotion is this?

A   advertising   C   sponsorship
B   point of sale   D   competition

13 A clothes retailer claims to have reduced its prices by 50 per cent when in fact they have been reduced by 10 per cent. Which of the following laws is it breaking?

    A Sale of Goods Act
    B Trade Descriptions Act
    C Consumer Protection Act
    D Consumer Credit Act

14 A company asks a cricket team to wear its name on their shirts and in return it agrees to pay the club's running costs. This is an example of:

    A point of sale   C competition
    B sponsorship   D advertisement

15 A company runs a poster campaign. This is offensive to a large section of the population. This campaign would be stopped by:

    A Trading Standards Office
    B Advertising Standards Authority
    C Consumer Protection Act
    D no one

16 Which of the following would most likely be used to inform people about the opening of a new supermarket in their locality?

    A sponsorship   C local press advert
    B competition   D national TV advert

17 Which of the following would most likely be used by a group of nurses who wished to raise money for a charity by swimming 500 metres?

    A sponsorship   C local press advert
    B competition   D national TV advert

Focus three: Providing customer service

18 If a customer has a complaint which of the following actions is most appropriate?

    A tell the customer to send a written complaint
    B listen to the complaint and say what will/can be done
    C tell the customer he/she is wrong
    D ignore the customer and hope he/she will go away

Questions 19 to 21 relate to the importance of meeting customer needs.

      A   to attract new customers
      B   to retain existing customers
      C   to enhance the organisation's image
      D   to gain customer satisfaction

Which of the above relates to the following?

19   A supermarket sends information and money-off coupons to regular customers.

      A   B   C   D

20   The same supermarket advertises in local papers with money-off coupons.

      A   B   C   D

21   The supermarket makes sure that it opens an extra checkout to ensure people do not have to queue up for long.

      A   B   C   D

Questions 22 to 24 relate to monitoring customer satisfaction.

      A   marketing research
      B   speaking to customers on the premises
      C   suggestion box
      D   numbers of customers

Which of the above relates to the following?

22   Allowing customers the opportunity to make comments anonymously about the service they have received

      A   B   C   D

23   A supermarket wants to find out what customers think about the new layout of the store.

      A   B   C   D

24   A company sends out a questionnaire to a representative sample of customers to find out what they think about the company and its products.

      A   B   C   D

25   A customer bought a designer dress and was told that it was
     unique and handmade in the shop in London. The customer
     then found out that it was not unique or handmade and had
     been imported from abroad. Which of the following has been
     breached?

         A   Sale of Goods Act
         B   Trade Descriptions Act
         C   Consumer Protection Act
         D   statutory rights

26   A customer has bought a satellite receiver but does not know
     how it works. What does the customer need?

         A   a replacement   C   information
         B   a refund   D   a guarantee

27   A clothes shop allows its customers to return any item that
     they are not completely satisfied with. Why does the shop
     allow this?

         A   to monitor sales levels
         B   to retain customers
         C   to get customer information
         D   to monitor customer levels

28   A supermarket wants to find out if its customers are happy
     with the service they get from the staff. Which of the following
     is best suited for this purpose? Ask the:

         A   staff to fill in a questionnaire
         B   supervisors to fill in a questionnaire
         C   customers to fill in a questionnaire
         D   manager to watch the customers

29   A customer has sent in a written complaint about a member
     of staff. Which of the following is best for the manager to use
     when making a formal reply?

         A   a memorandum   C   a complaints policy
         B   a report   D   a letter

30   A customer has bought a pair of shoes and a week later the
     sole has come apart. Which of the following would they use
     to get a refund or exchange the shoes?

         A   Sale of Goods Act
         B   Trade Descriptions Act
         C   Consumer Protection Act
         D   statutory rights

Consumers and Customers
Paper Two

Focus one: Importance of consumers and customers

Questions 1 to 3 relate to the following.

The buying habits of people will differ.

A   a pensioner couple
B   a middle-aged couple with teenage children
C   a young couple with very young children
D   a young couple with no children

Which of the following habits are most likely those of the above?

1   Taking a walking safari holiday

A   B   C   D

2   Taking a three- or four-month winter holiday in a warmer country

A   B   C   D

3   Worrying about buying school uniforms

A   B   C   D

4   Demand is most likely to decrease if one of the following happens.

A   decrease in unemployment
B   decrease in disposable income
C   decrease in interest rates
D   decrease in prices of goods

5   A food manufacturer wants to launch a new type of Mexican dish. Which of the following characteristics is it most likely to be interested in?

A   tastes   C   age
B   gender   D   fashion

6   A college of further education is considering whether it should provide special courses for people who wish to learn English as a second language. Which characteristic would be of interest to it?

A	tastes	C	gender
B	age	D	ethnicity

7 If consumers are spending more of their income, as a percentage, on basic goods, which of the following is most likely to have increased?

A the cost of living
B the earnings
C the level of employment
D the disposable income

8 Health-conscious consumers feel that white meat is healthier than red meat. How will the sales of red meat be affected?

A	demand will be unchanged	C	demand will decrease
B	demand will increase	D	demand will be constant

9 A supplier is most likely to increase production under one of the following circumstances. Which one?

A when disposable incomes decrease
B when demand is strong
C when demand is weak
D when tax is increased

10 The population of this country is ageing. Which of the following is most likely to see an increase?

A	adventure holidays	C	white water rafting
B	health service	D	bungee jumping

11 There is an increasing trend in people going to the cinema. How will this affect the sales/rental of video films?

A	increased demand	C	demand will be unaffected
B	decreased demand		
		D	there is no link

Focus two: Types of promotion in business

12 A sports shop dealing exclusively with golfing equipment would be advised to advertise:

A	in the national press	C	in specialist magazines
B	on national TV	D	on local radio

13 Which of the following would deal with complaints about press advertisements?

A ACAS   C ASA
B CBI   D ITC

14 Whose responsibility is it to investigate complaints that a shop is selling dangerous products?

A Trading Standards Office
B Health and Safety Executive
C Department of Trade and Industry
D social services

15 A supermarket arranges a wine-tasting session in store for customers. Which of the following promotions is it using?

A sponsorship   C press advertisement
B point of sale   D competition

16 A large brewery wants to encourage people to drink more of its products, but does not want people to drink and drive. It therefore decides to pay for all bus services on new year's eve. Which type of promotion is it using?

A sponsorship   C press advertisement
B point of sale   D competition

17 A large company wants to enhance its image and to be seen as a company that cares about the world in which it operates. Which of the following would be best suited to achieve its aims?

A a donation to the local golf club
B a donation to a recycling project
C a donation to a political party
D a donation to a working men's social club

Focus three: Providing customer service

Questions 18 to 20 relate to the following needs of customers.

A to obtain information
B to obtain a refund
C to exchange an item
D to be treated with courtesy

Which of the above relate to the following?

18   A customer wants her money back because the item she
     bought does not work.

      A   B   C   D

19   A customer wants to know more about an extended warranty
     scheme.

      A   B   C   D

20   A man has been given a shirt as a present, but it is the wrong
     size. He needs a bigger size.

      A   B   C   D

Questions 21 to 23 relate to the following Acts of Parliament.

    A   Sale of Goods Act
    B   Consumer Protection Act
    C   Trade Descriptions Act
    D   Health and Safety at Work Act

Which of the above laws would apply in the following
situations?

21   A shopkeeper sells a computer claiming it has the latest
     pentium chip, whereas it has an older 386 chip.

      A   B   C   D

22   The same shopkeeper also sells products that are not 'fit for
     their purpose'.

      A   B   C   D

23   The shopkeeper misleads customers by displaying a low price
     and then charging a higher one.

      A   B   C   D

24   The chief executive of a large chain of DIY stores wants to
     get first-hand experience of how staff treat customers. Which
     of the following would be most suitable?

    A   arrange a survey among staff
    B   carry out a survey among customers
    C   pretend to be a customer
    D   set up a meeting with all the staff

Questions 25 to 27 relate to the following methods of communication.

A	letter	C	face to face (oral)
B	memo	D	telephone

Which of these would be most suitable in the following situations?

25 To respond to a written complaint from a customer

A   B   C   D

26 To make a written request to a colleague to deal with a customer's problem

A   B   C   D

27 To ask a customer to come and pick up items that had been ordered

A   B   C   D

28 A customer has written to a company asking for information about its range of products and prices. Which of the following would be a suitable response?

A	a memo and catalogue	C	a mission statement
B	a letter and catalogue	D	an internal costs list

29 A customer has purchased a pair of new jeans. The first time they are worn the sides split. Which of the following Acts protects the customer?

A	Consumer Credit Act	C	Consumer Protection Act
B	Sale of Goods Act	D	Trade Descriptions Act

30 Say whether each of the following statements is true or false.

i)   Organisations may be legally liable for injuries to customers caused on their premises.

ii) The Consumer Protection Act requires organisations to take out public liability insurance.

A	True	True	C	False	True
B	True	False	D	False	False

Consumers and Customers
Paper Three

Focus one: Importance of consumers and customers

1   A motoring organisation plans to launch a new type of service which will give priority to women drivers. Which of the following characteristics are they most likely to be interested in?

    A   tastes   C   age
    B   gender   D   fashion

2   People who have low disposable income are most likely to buy more of the following products:

    A   luxury products   C   consumer durables
    B   food and clothes   D   exotic holidays

Questions 3 to 5 relate to the following reasons why demand for goods changes.

    A   confidence to spend   C   changing wants
    B   changing needs   D   advertising

Which of the above affects the following?

3   An increase in demand for luxury products such as four-wheel-drive vehicles and camcorders

    A   B   C   D

4   Young couples who have new babies

    A   B   C   D

5   Young people who tend to follow the latest fashion

    A   B   C   D

6   Say whether each of the following statements is true or false.

    i)   An increase in the sale of non-alcoholic lagers has resulted from people's concern about the dangers of drinking and driving.

    ii)   People's concern about the environment has resulted in a decrease in the sale of unleaded petrol.

    A   True   True   C   False   True
    B   True   False   D   False   False

7　A company that runs nursing homes for senior citizens would be most interested in one of the following categories. Which?

    A　geographical   C　age
    B　lifestyle   D　gender

8　Many families now buy increasing numbers of ready prepared meals. The main reason for this is:

    A　an increase in the number of housewives
    B　an increase in women working full time
    C　a decrease in women working full time
    D　an increase in male full-time employment

9　A clothes manufacturing company will see a decrease in sales if:

    A　it ensures high level of quality control
    B　it fails to keep up with changing tastes
    C　it changes products in line with fashion
    D　it monitors consumer tastes and acts on the result

10　Say whether each of the following statements is true or false.

    i)　People who have job security will have higher levels of confidence to spend compared with those who don't.

    ii)　People's buying habits will change as their family circumstances alter.

    A　True　True   C　False　True
    B　True　False   D　False　False

11　An insurance company wants to launch a school fees savings plan. Which characteristic would it be most concerned with?

    A　gender   C　lifestyle
    B　age   D　geographical

Focus two: Types of promotion in business

Questions 12 to 14 relate to the following types of promotion.

    A　point of sale
    B　posters at local bus stops
    C　sponsorship
    D　competition

Which of the above would be most suitable in the following cases?

12 A company wants to promote its new product by giving some away as prizes.

     A   B   C   D

13 A supermarket chain wants an in-store promotion.

     A   B   C   D

14 A cigarette company offers to pay the prize money for a televised snooker championship.

     A   B   C   D

15 Say whether each of the following statements is true or false.

i) The Trade Descriptions Act applies only to manu-facturers.

ii) Estate agents, as service providers, are exempt from the Trade Descriptions Act.

A	True	True	C	False	True
B	True	False	D	False	False

16 Say whether each of the following statements is true or false.

i) The Advertising Standards Authority is responsible for ensuring that poster advertisements are decent.

ii) The Trading Standards Office could take action against those companies selling unsafe products.

A	True	True	C	False	True
B	True	False	D	False	False

17 A computer superstore has arranged a demonstration of the latest software and hardware in the store for customers. Which of the following promotions is it using?

A	sponsorship	C	point of sale
B	press advertisement	D	competition

Focus three: Providing customer service

18 Which of the following may be a reason for investing in improved customer service?

    A increased sales performance
    B to clear stock due to bankruptcy
    C decreased sales performance
    D to improve staff morale

Questions 19 to 21 relate to the following customer needs.

    A   special needs
    B   to make a purchase
    C   to make a complaint
    D   to be able to return a faulty item

Which of the above relate to the following?

19 A customer who has purchased a radio and it does not function

    A   B   C   D

20 A customer who needs wheelchair access

    A   B   C   D

21 A customer who has been discriminated against

    A   B   C   D

22 A company puts out an advert for a product which gives a misleading price. Which of the following Acts is being breached?

    A   Sale of Goods Act
    B   Consumer Credit Act
    C   Consumer Protection Act
    D   Trade Descriptions Act

23 Satisfying the needs of customers is likely to result in one of the following:

    A   higher levels of repeat business
    B   higher levels of complaints
    C   higher levels of customer dissatisfaction
    D   increasing numbers of customers turning to competitors

24 Which of the following legislation requires organisations to take precautions against customers being injured on the premises?

    A   Consumer Protection Act
    B   Health and Safety at Work Act
    C   Trade Descriptions Act
    D   There is no Act to cover this

25 Say whether each of the following statements is true or false.

i)   Improving customer services is something that only loss-making organisations need to consider.

ii) The service that an organisation offers its clients can only be enhanced if all staff cooperate.

A True   True   C False True
B True   False   D False False

26 Say whether each of the following statements is true or false.

i)   The most reliable way to monitor customer satisfaction is to observe customers when they are shopping.

ii) Monitoring the trend in the level of sales over a period may show if there is a deterioration in customer service.

A True   True   C False True
B True   False   D False False

Questions 27 to 29 relate to the following communications methods.

A telephone   C statement of account
B letter   D price list

Which of the above apply to the following?

27 To give to customers who want to know the costs for a range of products

A   B   C   D

28 To inform a customer about his/her debt for products purchased on credit

A   B   C   D

29 To respond to a customer's query verbally

A   B   C.   D

30 Which Act of Parliament requires that goods sold must be of 'satisfactory quality'?

A Health and Safety at Work Act
B Sale of Goods Act
C Consumer Protection Act
D Trade Descriptions Act

Consumers and Customers
Paper Four

Focus one: Importance of consumers and customers

Questions 1 to 3 relate to the following reasons why demand for goods changes.

A	confidence to spend	C	changing wants
B	changing needs	D	advertising

Which of the above affects the following?

1   An increasing number of people are choosing to rent rather than buy their own homes.

   A   B   C   D

2   Product promotions which seek to influence people's buying habits

   A   B   C   D

3   An increase in the sale of health foods

   A   B   C   D

4   Consumers are prepared to pay slightly higher prices for environmentally friendly products. This has resulted in an increased supply of

   A   non-degradable plastics
   B   leaded petrol
   C   recyclable products
   D   fossil fuel

5   A company wants to launch a new product and wishes to promote it region by region. Which characteristic will it find most useful?

   A   age   C   fashion
   B   gender   D   geographical

6   In which of the following circumstances would a manufacturer increase supply?

   A   when demand is strong
   B   when demand is weak
   C   when VAT is increased
   D   when demand is stagnant

7   Middle-class retired couples are most likely to buy which of the following combination of products?

    A   household goods and children's clothes
    B   household goods and winter holidays
    C   household goods and adventure holidays
    D   household goods and pop music records

8   There has been a trend over the last few years for more people to become vegetarians. Which of the following best describes the effect of the trend?

    A   decrease in purchase of non-meat products
    B   increase in purchase of non-meat products
    C   increase in purchase of meat products
    D   decrease in meat promotion

9   Demand is likely to be weak when:

    A   VAT has decreased
    B   disposable income has increased
    C   unemployment has increased
    D   confidence to spend has increased

10   If consumers are spending more of their income, as a percentage, on non-basic goods, which of the following is most likely to have decreased?

    A   the cost of living
    B   the earnings
    C   the level of employment
    D   the disposable income

11   In which of the following circumstances would a manufacturer decrease supply?

    A   when demand is strong
    B   when demand is weak
    C   when VAT is decreased
    D   when incomes are rising

Focus two: Types of promotion in business

Questions 12 to 14 relate to the following information

A	trade journal	C	talking pages
B	national press	D	local paper

Which of the above would be most suitable for the following situations?

12　Launch of a new consumer product

A　　B　　C　　D

13　A self-employed electrician available for domestic installations/repairs

A　　B　　C　　D

14　A new plumbing technique developed and now available

A　　B　　C　　D

15　A company launches a new shaving gel for men. How might it most effectively encourage men to try this product?

A	sell at half price	C	free samples
B	money off next purchase	D	a competition

16　Which of the following bodies has the power to deal with complaints about press advertisements?

A　Broadcasting Complaints Authority
B　Advertising Standards Authority
C　Trading Standards Office
D　Independent Television Commission

17　Which of the following situations would be least likely to give rise to bad publicity for a large company?

A　secret donations to a political party
B　pay freeze for workers and 30 per cent increase for MD
C　chief executive swims the channel
D　women challenge discriminatory promotion policy

Focus three: Providing customer service

18 A company continually strives to enhance its image and improve customer service. What benefit might it get from this?

    A become less competitive
    B attract new customers
    C improve its productivity
    D find out the numbers of customers

19 A large departmental store has failed to display fire exit signs. Which legislation requires them to do this?

    A Health and Safety at Work Act
    B Sale of Goods Act
    C Consumer Protection Act
    D Trade Descriptions Act

20 The Post Office wants to find out what customers think about the service they get. Which of the following would provide the most reliable results?

    A the manager should ask some customers about the service
    B questionnaires should be distributed among a large sample
    C monitor the number of complaints
    D monitor the number of compliments

Questions 21 to 23 relate to the following reasons for providing customer-service.

    A to gain new customers
    B to retain existing customers
    C to enhance organisation's image
    D to provide customer satisfaction

Which of the above relate to the following?

21 Sending details of special offers to regular customers

    A   B   C   D

22 Making donations to community projects

    A   B   C   D

23 Dealing with customer complaints swiftly

    A   B   C   D

Questions 24 to 26 relate to the following legislation.

> A Consumer Protection Act
> B Trade Descriptions Act
> C Sale of Goods Act
> D Health and Safety at Work Act

Which of the above legislation is being contravened in the following circumstances?

24 A company makes grand claims about its product which it knows to be untrue.

> A   B   C   D

25 A customer has bought a mountain bike and on the first day the frame collapses.

> A   B   C   D

26 A shop puts up 'sale' and 'prices slashed' posters but has not changed its prices at all.

> A   B   C   D

27 A customer has bought a new TV, but when the box is opened the customer sees that there are scratches all over the set. What does the customer need?

> A a replacement   C information
> B a refund   D a guarantee

Questions 28 to 30 relate to the following information.

> A national press   C women's magazine
> B national TV   D sales brochure

Which of the above would be used for the following?

28 To advertise a new range of eye shadow

> A   B   C   D

29 A company selling a new type of fertiliser to farmers

> A   B   C   D

30 To advertise a new product along with money-off coupons

> A   B   C   D

Consumers and Customers
Paper Five

Focus one: Importance of consumers and customers

1   A soft drinks manufacturer is interested in finding out which types of drink, of the ones that it makes, are preferred by pensioners.

Which of the following characteristics in the national population are they interested in?

  A age   C social class
  B sex   D income

2   The same drinks company wants to know in which parts of the country it sells most drinks. Which of the following characteristics is it interested in?

  A income   C fashion
  B geographical   D lifestyles

3   A company makes luxury products. Which type of customer is most likely to be targeted?

  A owners of houses only
  B low disposable income groups
  C high disposable income groups
  D teenagers

4   A newspaper reports that a certain type of illness may be linked to eating beef. What is the likely result of this going to be?

  A increase in beef sales
  B decrease in all meat sales
  C no change in beef sales
  D decrease in beef sales

5   Demand is likely to be strong when:

  A income tax has increased
  B disposable income has increased
  C purchase tax has increased
  D unemployment has increased

6　Say whether each of the following statements is true or false.

i)　Disposable income is the money that people have left after paying the rent and for shopping etc.

ii)　Disposable income can only be spent on leisure activities.

A　True　True　　　　　C　False　True
B　True　False　　　　 D　False　False

7　A company wants to launch a new product and wishes to promote it among the well off. Which characteristic will it find most useful?

A　age　　　　　　　　C　lifestyle
B　gender　　　　　　 D　geographical

8　There is an increasing trend for people to buy compact discs. How will this affect the sales of cassettes?

A　increased demand
B　decreased demand
C　demand will be unaffected
D　there is no link

Questions 9 to 11 relate to the following information.

The following can cause changes in demand for goods and services.

A　increase in cost of living
B　confidence to spend
C　advertising
D　changing wants

Which of the above applies to the following?

9　People spending more on necessary household items

A　　　B　　　C　　　D

10　An increase in the demand for skiing and other winter holidays

A　　　B　　　C　　　D

11　Being influenced by product promotions

A　　　B　　　C　　　D

Focus two: Types of promotion in business

12   A company launches a new hand cream for women. How might it most effectively encourage women to try this product?

    A sell at half price   C free samples
    B money off next   D a competition
       purchase

13   A farm machinery manufacturer would be best advised to promote its equipment:

    A on national television
    B in the national press
    C in a trade journal
    D on a London radio station

14   Many companies promote their name by having sports stars wear the company logo. How do they get the stars to wear them?

    A by lobbying them
    B by sponsoring them
    C by issuing press releases
    D by improving community relations

15   Many companies make large donations to charities and other good causes. What benefit might they get from this?

    A promotes sponsorship   C increases investment
    B promotes public image   D improves lobbying

16   An insurance company is most likely to use which of the following methods to promote and sell policies?

    A pyramid selling   C agents
    B catalogues   D a wholesaler

17   Marketing involves promoting products using various methods. Which of the following would be least likely to be used for a product that is sold in a particular geographical location?

    A posters in shops   C national television
    B local newspapers   D billboards

Focus three: Providing customer service

Questions 18 to 20 relate to the following.

> A door-to-door leaflets in a neighbourhood
> B posters on hoardings nationally
> C specialist journal
> D local TV advertisement

Which of the above communication methods would be most suitable for the following?

18 To announce the opening of a corner shop

> A   B   C   D

19 The development of a new type of hard disk for computers

> A   B   C   D

20 To raise general public awareness over a period about a forthcoming product, cost effectively

> A   B   C   D

21 Say whether each of the following statements is true or false.

i) Organisations cannot be held liable for injuries to customers caused on their premises as long as there are signs asking customers to be careful.

ii) The Consumer Protection Act requires organisations to take out public liability insurance.

> A True   True   C False True
> B True   False   D False False

Questions 22 to 24 relate to the following customer needs.

> A need for information
> B need for ethical standards
> C need for care and attention
> D need to complain

22 A cashier attempts to short-change a customer.

> A   B   C   D

23 An elderly customer is confused and cannot make up his mind about which item to buy.

> A   B   C   D

24   A customer is not sure what the main differences are between
     two video recorders.

       A   B   C   D

25   A company can assume its customer service is satisfactory
     when:

    A   it results in increased complaints
    B   it results in increased refunds
    C   it results in increased sales
    D   it results in decreased sales

Questions 26 to 28 relate to the following legislation.

    A   Trade Descriptions Act
    B   Sale of Goods Act
    C   Consumer Protection Act
    D   Health and Safety at Work Act

Which Act would apply in the following cases?

26   A washing powder manufacturer claims that its powder can
     remove all stains, when this is not quite true.

       A   B   C   D

27   Products must be 'fit for the purpose'.

       A   B   C   D

28   It is a criminal offence for a trader to sell unsafe goods.

       A   B   C   D

29   Say whether each of the following statements is true or false.

    i)   A business can monitor the success or failure of its
        customer service by carrying out market research.

    ii) A business can monitor the success or failure of its
        customer service by getting customer feedback.

    A   True   True   C   False   True
    B   True   False   D   False   False

30   Which Act of Parliament requires that a seller should not make
     misleading claims about his products?

    A   Health and Safety at Work Act
    B   Sale of Goods Act
    C   Consumer Protection Act
    D   Trade Descriptions Act

Chapter 3

Answers to Test Papers

Unit One: Business Organisations and Employment

Paper One (page 21)

1 A	2 C	3 A	4 C	5 B	6 C	7 B	8 C	9 B	10 B
11 D	12 C	13 D	14 B	15 B	16 C	17 A	18 C	19 A	20 C
21 D	22 B	23 A	24 C	25 B	26 C	27 D	28 C	29 B	30 C

Paper Two (page 26)

1 C	2 B	3 B	4 B	5 C	6 C	7 D	8 B	9 C	10 B
11 C	12 B	13 A	14 A	15 A	16 D	17 B	18 D	19 C	20 B
21 B	22 D	23 B	24 B	25 B	26 D	27 C	28 C	29 C	30 B

Paper Three (page 30)

1 B	2 B	3 B	4 A	5 B	6 B	7 C	8 B	9 B	10 B
11 C	12 B	13 B	14 C	15 C	16 B	17 C	18 A	19 C	20 A
21 A	22 C	23 B	24 C	25 B	26 A	27 D	28 B	29 B	30 C

Paper Four (page 35)

1 C	2 A	3 B	4 C	5 B	6 D	7 D	8 C	9 A	10 B
11 A	12 B	13 C	14 A	15 B	16 B	17 C	18 B	19 D	20 C
21 A	22 D	23 B	24 B	25 C	26 C	27 D	28 C	29 B	30 B

Paper Five (page 40)

1 C	2 C	3 B	4 A	5 A	6 C	7 A	8 C	9 C	10 B
11 B	12 B	13 C	14 B	15 B	16 A	17 D	18 B	19 C	20 B
21 B	22 B	23 B	24 B	25 A	26 B	27 B	28 C	29 C	30 B

Unit Two: People in Business Organisations

Paper One (page 45)

1 A	2 B	3 B	4 B	5 A	6 D	7 D	8 A	9 B	10 C
11 C	12 B	13 C	14 B	15 D	16 D	17 D	18 D	19 D	20 B
21 B	22 C	23 B	24 C	25 B	26 A	27 B	28 D	29 C	30 C

Paper Two (page 50)

1 B	2 B	3 A	4 D	5 D	6 A	7 C	8 A	9 D	10 C
11 C	12 C	13 B	14 A	15 D	16 B	17 C	18 D	19 B	20 C
21 C	22 B	23 C	24 A	25 B	26 D	27 C	28 B	29 B	30 B

Paper Three (page 55)

1 C	2 B	3 A	4 C	5 B	6 C	7 B	8 C	9 B	10 C
11 D	12 D	13 C	14 D	15 B	16 A	17 C	18 B	19 C	20 C
21 D	22 B	23 C	24 A	25 C	26 B	27 A	28 A	29 C	30 D

Paper Four (page 60)

1 C	2 D	3 A	4 D	5 C	6 D	7 A	8 B	9 C	10 B
11 B	12 A	13 D	14 C	15 D	16 C	17 A	18 C	19 C	20 B
21 D	22 C	23 B	24 D	25 B	26 A	27 C	28 D	29 D	30 B

Paper Five (page 65)

1 A	2 B	3 D	4 A	5 C	6 A	7 B	8 D	9 B	10 B
11 A	12 B	13 D	14 C	15 D	16 B	17 C	18 A	19 B	20 A
21 D	22 C	23 C	24 D	25 D	26 C	27 D	28 A	29 B	30 A

Unit Three: Consumers and Customers

Paper One (page 71)

1 A	2 B	3 D	4 C	5 C	6 A	7 C	8 B	9 A	10 C
11 C	12 B	13 C	14 B	15 B	16 C	17 A	18 B	19 B	20 A
21 D	22 C	23 B	24 A	25 B	26 C	27 B	28 C	29 D	30 A

Paper Two (page 76)

1 D	2 A	3 B	4 B	5 A	6 D	7 A	8 C	9 B	10 B
11 B	12 C	13 C	14 A	15 B	16 A	17 B	18 B	19 A	20 C
21 C	22 A	23 B	24 C	25 A	26 B	27 D	28 B	29 B	30 B

Paper Three (page 81)

1 B	2 B	3 A	4 B	5 C	6 B	7 C	8 B	9 B	10 A
11 C	12 D	13 A	14 C	15 D	16 A	17 C	18 C	19 D	20 A
21 C	22 C	23 A	24 B	25 C	26 C	27 D	28 C	29 A	30 B

Paper Four (page 86)

1 A	2 D	3 C	4 C	5 D	6 A	7 B	8 B	9 C	10 A
11 B	12 B	13 D	14 A	15 C	16 B	17 C	18 B	19 A	20 B
21 B	22 C	23 D	24 B	25 C	26 A	27 A	28 C	29 D	30 A

Paper Five (page 91)

1 A	2 B	3 C	4 D	5 B	6 D	7 C	8 B	9 A	10 B
11 C	12 C	13 C	14 B	15 B	16 C	17 C	18 A	19 C	20 B
21 D	22 B	23 C	24 A	25 C	26 A	27 B	28 C	29 A	30 D

Chapter 4

Glossary of Business and Related Terms

Absolute monopoly A situation whereby a single producer or supplier has control of the entire output of a commodity or service. This is very rare in real life. Also referred to as pure monopoly.

ACAS (Advisory, Conciliation and Arbitration Service) A service that is funded by the government and used to resolve industrial disputes. ACAS also provides advisory services to employers, employees and trade unions on work and employment issues.

Account payee The words found on a cheque indicate that it should be paid only into the bank or building society account of the person to whom it is made payable.

Accountant A person who is qualified in the subject of accounts.

Accounting The recording of a company's transactions in the appropriate manner, using acknowledged methods and conventions.

Administration system A system which supports a business and its functions. The system can be manual or computerised.

Ad valorem Latin for 'according to value'. That is, as a percentage. See *Ad valorem tax*.

Ad valorem tax A duty imposed on products and services in proportion to their value, ie a duty expressed as a percentage and not a flat amount.

Advertising Standards Authority (ASA) An independent organisation which deals with complaints from the public about advertisements in newspapers, magazines and on billboards.

Advisory, Conciliation and Arbitration Service See *ACAS*.

After-sales service Back-up services provided by suppliers for the benefit of their customers. These could include on-site repairs or a 24-hour telephone help line.

Annual General Meeting (AGM) A meeting of the shareholders of a limited liability company that must be held yearly, as required by law. The purpose is to allow shareholders to discuss their company's annual report and accounts, elect directors and agree the dividend payout.

Application package A pre-written program, or suite of programs, which carries out a particular task, eg a word processing program.

Applications software See *Application package*.

Articles of Association This document determines the internal constitution of the company. It has to be submitted to the *Registrar of Companies* when seeking registration of a company. The Articles cover such matters as borrowing powers, appointments and power of directors, shareholders' meetings and voting rights.

ASA See *Advertising Standards Authority*.

Assets The property that belongs to a business, such as cash, stock, buildings, machinery and even things such as goodwill or patents. See *Current assets* and *Fixed assets*.

Assurance An agreement between an individual and an insurance company, whereby the individual pays premiums at regular intervals in return for a sum of money to be received at a later date, when a certain event will assuredly take place, eg death. See *Insurance*.

Auditor A professional accountant who checks, when appointed, the accuracy of a company's annual report and accounts. The auditor then has to present an independent report to shareholders on whether the accounts represent a true and fair view of the company's affairs.

Back-up copy A duplicate of data or computer programs used to restore the original if it is lost or destroyed.

BACS (Bankers Automated Clearing Service) This system allows the transfer of money, by computer link, between banks and building societies. Customers' standing orders and direct debits, for example, are paid using this system.

Bad debt Where a company is owed money by its customers or borrowers and is unlikely to be paid because, for example, the customer has become insolvent.

Balance of payments The difference between the payments of all kinds made from one country to the rest of the world and its receipts from all other countries.

Balance of trade The difference between the value of a country's imports and exports. A surplus on the balance of trade is where the cost of imports is less then the earnings from exports.

Balance sheet An accounting statement of a firm's *assets* and liabilities on the last day of a trading period. This is normally produced on a yearly basis.

Bank rate See *Base rate*.

Bankruptcy See *Insolvency*.

Base rate Usually, the basic rate for lending by a bank. Also referred to as a bank rate.

Batch processing The processing of data accumulated over a period of time, ie batched. The user cannot further influence processing while it is in progress.

Bi-directional printer A type of printer that prints in both directions, from left to right and the next line right to left, thus increasing printing speed.

Black economy See *Cash economy*.

Boom A period of expansion of business activity. The opposite of slump or recession. A boom reaches a peak when the economy is working at full capacity.

Bootstrap A program used to start (or 'boot') the computer, usually by clearing the primary memory, setting up various devices, and loading the operating system from secondary storage or ROM.

Branding (marketing term) The process of differentiating a product in the eyes of the consumer, eg soap powder.

Break-even analysis Analysis undertaken by a business to establish the point at which sales revenue is equal to the total expenses; at that point profit (and loss) is zero.

Break-even point The point at which a business is making neither a profit nor a loss. At this point revenue is equal to expenditure.

Broadcasting Complaints Commission Created in 1981, the Commission will consider complaints made about, to do with unjust or unfair treatment regarding, or to do with unwarranted infringement of privacy in obtaining material included in, a radio or television broadcast.

Budget A company's plan, usually expressed in financial terms, for a given future period, of how much is to be spent and on what.

Bug A defect or malfunction in a computer program or system.

Building society A financial institution which specialises in the provision of long-term mortgage loans for the purchase of a property. In recent years they have also been offering their customers some banking services such as cheque books, credit cards, direct debits etc.

Bureaucracy A structured organisation formed to achieve specific goals. Its features include: clearly defined jobs; a hierarchy; a set of rules to govern operations; employees who are appointed (not elected) to posts; and a system of promotion.

Business organisation Where a group of people come together and interact with one another to achieve a set of pre-determined goals, usually with profit as the main objective.

Business plan A document setting out what the business is, what it aims to achieve, and how it intends to achieve it. There is no set format for producing a business plan; however, it is often set out in five sections. These are: Objectives, Marketing Plan, Production Plan, Resources Needed, Financial Projections.

CAD Computer-Aided Design.

CAL Computer-Assisted Learning.

CAM Computer-Aided Manufacturing.

Capital A term used to describe the various components – money, equipment etc – used in a business.

Capital expenditure Money used to purchase or to improve *fixed assets*.

Cash economy Here all trade is carried out for payment in cash only, where taxes or other duties such as VAT are not paid. This type of activity is also referred to as the hidden economy, black economy, underground economy or moonlight economy.

Cash flow The money that comes into and goes out of a business enterprise.

Cash flow forecast A forecast of the money expected to flow into and out of the business over a given period, usually one year.

Cash flow statement A statement showing the amounts of money that are likely to flow into and flow out of the business over a period.

CBT Computer-Based Training.

CD-ROM Compact Disk Read-Only Memory.

Cell Where a column and row intersect in a spreadsheet, that is known as a cell.

Central bank A bank which in any country is 1. banker to the government, 2. banker to the commercial banks, and 3. implements the currency and credit policy of the country. The Bank of England is the central bank for the UK.

Central Processing Unit The nerve-centre of the computer, which consists of the control unit, the arithmetic and logic unit and the main store.

Certificate of Incorporation The *Registrar of Companies* issues a certificate to a new company whose Memorandum of Association and *Articles of Association* are acceptable. Once incorporated, the company is a legal entity and can enter into contracts in its own name.

Chamber of Commerce An organisation which operates to serve the needs and for the benefit of the business community.

Cheque An instruction to a banker to pay a stated sum of money to the person to whom the cheque is made payable (the payee). Current legislation demands that all cheques are paid through a payee's account.

Cheque guarantee card A card issued to account holders. The issuing bank will guarantee payment up to a certain limit even if there is no money in the account.

Chief executive The person with the overall responsibility for the management of a company or firm. The term Managing

Director is often used in place of Chief Executive, as both are similar in terms of responsibility for the running of a company.

Chip (silicon) A tiny piece of semiconducting material which holds tens of thousands of electronic circuits.

Collective bargaining Where the employers and the representative of the workforce, for example a trade union, negotiate to determine the rates of pay, conditions of employment etc. The desired outcome of collective bargaining is a collective agreement.

Command economy Descriptive of an economic system dominated by central planning, as distinct from a free enterprise economy with a minimum of state interference.

Company secretary An officer of a *limited liability* company with responsibility for maintaining the company's share register, for notifying shareholders of annual general meetings and for preparing the company's annual return, as well as ensuring compliance with company law.

Computer A set of machines, controlled by an internally stored program, which accepts raw data and outputs information.

Confederation of British Industry (CBI) The representative organisation of British industry. The Confederation seeks to express the views of industry as a whole and to offer advice to the government on all aspects of policy which affect the interests of industry.

Consumer A person who uses a product. This person may not be the customer, ie the buyer. Parents may buy products for their children – the consumers.

Consumer Credit Act 1974 This Act requires persons or businesses who are engaged in the provision of consumer credit to be licensed. The Act is aimed at moneylenders, pawnbrokers and Instalment Credit traders but not banks as they are covered by other legislation. The Act also gives rights to borrowers.

Consumer durable A product of reasonably long life, such as a fridge or furniture, as distinct from, say, foodstuffs.

Consumer goods Products in the actual form in which they will reach domestic consumers.

Consumer Protection Act 1987 This Act gives protection to consumers in that it requires any goods sold or displayed to comply with the general safety requirement.

Control unit The part of the CPU which fetches program instructions from the main store, interprets them, and then causes the other hardware elements to function.

Cooperative A business where members join together to run a business for their own benefit and have equal shares in it.

Corporation tax A direct tax paid by companies on the profit of the business.

Cost-benefit analysis A comparison between the cost of carrying out a service or activity and the value of that service or activity, quantifying, as far as possible, all costs and benefits whether direct or indirect, financial or social.

CPU See *Central Processing Unit*.

Credit card A card provided by financial institutions such as banks and building societies. Customers who have this card are able to purchase goods and services or withdraw cash up to an agreed limit. The customers then have an option to pay the card issuer the whole amount owed at the end of the month or to make a minimum payment of 5 per cent of the outstanding balance.

Credit control The control that a company exercises to ensure that customers pay their debts on time and to minimise the risk of *bad debts*. Effective credit control minimises the amount of money that is tied up in *debtors*, so improving profitability and liquidity.

Credit note A note issued by a supplier to a customer who may have been overcharged or have returned goods. The note will show the amount that is owed to the customer.

Creditor A person or company who is owed money for supplying products or services.

Current assets These would consist of cash, stock and book debts.

Current liabilities The debts of the business which have to be paid within a year.

Curriculum vitae (CV) A document which details an individual's life history, with the emphasis on qualifications and employment.

Customer A person who buys a product. See *Consumer*.

Customs and Excise A government department concerned with the administration and collection of revenue from VAT, excise duties and customs duties.

Customs duty A duty or tax that is levied by the government on some imported products, ie foreign goods.

Data The raw facts and figures which arise from the day-to-day activities of an organisation. These do not in themselves allow any meaningful decisions to be made. However, when data is processed, information is produced.

Database A consolidated file which holds the data relating either to the whole of an organisation's operations or to a major operational area. Databases are also known as data banks; they use the concept of the integrated file.

Data capture The gathering of data at its source for direct input to a computer system.

Data collection The gathering together of data prior to its input to a computer system.

Data item The smallest element of data stored or used by a program.

Data pad A pressure-sensitive pad which allows a user to write on a blank form and thereby enter data into a computer.

Data processing Operations performed on raw *data* to produce meaningful information.

Data Protection Act Introduced in 1984 to give certain rights to individuals, such as access to information held on computer about them. The main purpose is to protect data subjects, individuals whose information is held on computer. The information must be electronically processed; if it is held on paper-based files the Act does not apply.

Data Protection Registrar The official responsible for maintaining a register of companies which hold information about people on computer.

Debentures Long-term fixed interest loans to companies. Interest is payable on these stocks whether or not a profit is earned. Debenture stockholders rank as *creditors* of the company.

Debit card A card issued by banks and building societies to customers to allow them to make payments from their accounts. The debit card works in the same way as a cheque. If you make a payment then your account is debited. The use of a debit card means that a cheque does not have to be written out. A debit card transaction is handled in a similar way to a credit card transaction.

Debit note A document issued to a customer, by a supplier, charging the customer for any additional goods or services supplied to them for which payment has not been received.

Debtor A person or company that owes money to another person or company. The opposite of *creditor*.

Debug The process of detecting and eliminating errors in a computer program or a system.

Dedicated word processor A machine that can only be used as a word processor; it cannot run other programs such as spreadsheets or databases, as a general purpose computer can.

Delivery note A document that is given to a customer when goods are delivered; it lists the items supplied. The customer can therefore check it against what has been received.

Demand The amount of a good or service that will be bought at any given price per unit of time.

Demand price The price which buyers are prepared to pay for a given quantity of a good or service.

Demerger Where a company (originally formed through a merger) is broken up into two or more parts.

Demographic trends A description of movements and changes in the population of a nation caused by such factors as immigration, emigration, age and gender distribution, level of education and so on.

Depreciation The sum of money that is written off the book value of a *fixed asset*. This is charged as an expense in the profit and loss account.

Desk research Information obtained from already published sources.

Desk-top publishing (DTP) Computer-aided publishing that uses equipment small enough to fit on a desk-top or table and suitable for an *end user*.

Diagnostic program A program designed to detect and locate faults in a computer.

Dialogue In a *WIMP* environment, a small on-screen box that invites the user to enter a response to a query, an option, or other information.

Direct debit Here the account holder authorises the person or company to whom he is indebted to arrange with his bank for the required regular payments to be transferred from the account. The amount that is transferred each month does not have to be a fixed sum, as is the case with a standing order.

Direct marketing Goods or services are sold direct to the customer without intermediaries, for example by mail order catalogues or direct mail.

Directory A named grouping of files on a disk that is recognised by the operating system.

Discrimination The act of treating a person or a group of persons unfairly, perhaps because of their gender, race, nationality, religion etc.

Disk or **Diskette** A flat, circular plate with a magnetisable surface layer on which data can be stored by magnetic recording.

Disk drive A device that houses a disk or diskette while it is in use. It contains a motor and one or more magnetic heads to read and write data on the disk.

Disposable income The amount of money a person has after deductions of income tax, national insurance and pension contributions. The amount of disposable income is important because this affects people's ability to purchase goods and services.

Diversification Whereby firms move into different markets or products in order to spread risk and thus reduce over-dependency on one market or product.

Dividend The portion of a company's profits which share-holders decide to distribute to ordinary shareholders each year.

DOS A program which controls the information in the computer (Disk Operating System).

Dot-matrix printer A printer or a plotter that prints characters or line images that are represented by dots. Synonymous with matrix printer.

Double-density disk A disk that can hold twice as much information as a single-density disk.

Double-sided disk A disk that can hold information on both sides.

Down time The length of time for which a computer system cannot be used due to a malfunction, or to maintenance being carried out.

DTI (Department of Trade and Industry) A government department whose prime function is to implement and administer the government's industrial and trade policies.

DTP See *Desk-top publishing*.

EDI (Electronic Data Interchange) A system which transfers commercial and administrative instructions between computers using agreed formats for the messages.

Effective demand Demand measured by spending on consumption (goods and services). For effective demand consumers must have the ability to pay, otherwise it is merely a desire.

EFTPOS (Electronic Funds Transfer at Point of Sale) A system which allows a retailer to debit the bank account or credit card account of the purchaser at the point of sale, and at the same time to credit the retailer's account.

Elasticity The extent to which a change in price will affect demand for a product. If a given price change produces a significant change in demand for a commodity, it is termed 'elastic', if there is no change then it is termed 'inelastic'.

Elasticity of supply The response of supply to a change in price of a product or service. If the price rises the amount supplied will normally be increased.

Electronic mail The transmission of messages among computer users over a data communication network. There is usually a 'mail box' where messages are stored until retrieved.

Employee A person who works for an individual or organisation (company, government, etc) on a paid basis to carry out a job or work task specified in his/her contract of employment.

Employer An organisation (company, government, etc) or person who engages employees (workers) to carry out a job or work task for pay.

Employers' liability insurance The law requires that employers take out insurance to cover employees against injury or death at work.

Employment contract A document which details the main terms and conditions of the job; not all the rights and obligations of the employer and employee will be written down – some will be implied.

Employment Protection (consolidation) Act 1978 This Act brought together a number of other Acts of parliament which were passed to give protection to employees. For example, not to be dismissed unfairly, and to receive an itemised payslip.

End users 1. People who ultimately use application software. 2. Users of a product (rather than purchasers).

Equal Opportunities Commission As a result of the passing of the Sex Discrimination Act 1975, The Equal Opportunities Commission was set up with the remit of: working towards the elimination of sex discrimination in education, employment and consumer services; promoting equality of opportunity; monitoring the effectiveness of the Sex Discrimination and Equal Pay Act.

Equilibrium The point at which demand and supply is equal. For example, a market is in equilibrium when, at the ruling price, the amount of goods or services being offered for sale is just equal to the amount consumers wish to buy.

Ergonomics The science of designing, among other things, computer hardware and software to make them more easy and comfortable for users.

Error A mistake or a fault that prevents the program or system from running as expected.

Error message Indicates that an error has occurred.

Exchange rate This can be thought of as the price of one currency in terms of another. In other words, how many pounds sterling or another currency do you have to pay for, say, US dollars or any other currency.

Excise duty An indirect tax imposed on a product, such as tobacco, alcoholic drinks and petrol, by the government. The demand for these products is highly price-inelastic.

Export Goods and services produced in one country and sent abroad to be sold. Goods are a visible export whereas services are an invisible export.

Facsimile transmission (fax) The transmission of a copy of a document via a telecommunication link. Both text and graphics can be transmitted.

Factors of production The various agents which combine to produce goods and services. Land, labour and capital are the traditional categories.

Field On a data medium or in storage, a specified area used for a particular class of data; for example, a group of character positions used to enter or display wage rates on a screen.

File A set of related records treated as a unit; for example, in stock control, a file could consist of a set of *invoices*. Another example could be a personnel file.

Fiscal policy The regulation of government spending and taxation to control the level of spending in the economy.

Fixed assets These include such things as buildings and machinery that are bought for long-term use in a firm rather than for resale.

Fixed costs Costs which tend to be unaffected by variations in the volume of output. For example, rent is a fixed cost.

Floppy disk See *Disk*.

Flow chart A graphical representation in which symbols are used to represent such things as operations, data, flow direction, and equipment for the definition, analysis, or solution of a problem, Synonymous with flow diagram.

Font A family or assortment of characters of a given size and style of printing type: for example, Times Roman.

Font cartridge A cartridge that can be plugged in to a printer to increase or add new fonts to a printer.

Forecasting The process of using qualitative and quantitative data to estimate future outcomes such as sales, costs and market share.

Formatting (a disk) To put the magnetic track and sector pattern on a disk, which is needed before the disk can store any information. Formatting completely erases any previously stored data.

Franchise A situation whereby a person purchases the right to use a well-known business name and possibly know-how as well. The franchisee (the buyer) will also have to pay a royalty – a percentage of the profits.

Free market economy Where there is no government intervention (in theory) and prices are determined by the forces of demand and supply.

Fringe benefit A benefit that is offered to employees over and above their wage or salary, for example luncheon vouchers, company car, share option scheme, non-contributory pension scheme.

GATT (General Agreement on Tariffs and Trade) An international organisation established to promote the expansion of international trade through the removal of tariffs and other restrictions on cross-border trade.

Gigabyte One billion bytes.

Golden handshake Whereby an employee is offered a generous severance payment to leave an organisation. Also sometimes used to describe payments made to retiring employees as a sign of gratitude for their services.

Golden hello Usually a large lump-sum payment made to an employee as an inducement to join an organisation.

Grandparent-parent-child back-up A file back-up system in which the current version and the two previous versions of a file are always retained.

Grievance A complaint by an employee arising out of his/her employment. The grievance may be against the employer or another member of staff.

Grievance procedure A set of rules stating the procedures to be followed when an employee has a complaint arising out of his/her employment. It is a legal requirement that employees other than those in small firms be notified in writing (with the contract of employment), of the steps they can take if they have a grievance.

Gross Domestic Product (GDP) The total of all goods and services produced in an economy over a one-year period, in monetary terms.

Gross National Product (GNP) A measure of a nation's output, the GDP, plus income from abroad such as profits, dividends, rent and interest.

Gross profit The profit before expenses are deducted. The difference between sales and the cost of sales.

Hacker A person who attempts to break into secure computer systems, or is interested in doing so. Hacking is a criminal activity.

Hard copy A printed copy of machine output in a visually readable form; for example, printed reports, listings, documents and summaries.

Hard disk Used for storing information, similar to a floppy disk, but has greater capacity and is housed inside the computer.

Hardware The devices that make up a computer. See *Software*.

Health and Safety at Work Act 1974 This Act requires employers to have a written safety policy. It also places an obligation on employees to observe safety rules, and allows for the appointment of trade union safety representatives.

Health and Safety Executive The Health and safety at Work Act established the Health and Safety Executive to enforce the provisions of the 1974 Act.

Hierarchical organisation An organisation with a series of levels of authority.

High-density disk A disk that is able to hold a greater amount of information than a *double-sided disk*.

Hire purchase A method of purchasing goods whereby the buyer pays an initial deposit and agrees to pay the balance in equal parts over a set period. The buyer does not become the legal owner until the whole balance has been paid.

Hypermedia Software in which pictures, music and text may be linked to create a presentation.

Icon A small pictorial symbol in a *WIMP* environment, representing a program option, which can be selected by clicking on it with a mouse.

Impact printer A printer which uses physical contact with the paper.

Income tax A tax paid on the income of individuals (wages, dividends, interest rent).

Income tax allowance (or **Personal allowance**) The amount of income a person is allowed before beginning to pay income tax.

Independent Television Commission A statutory body which oversees and controls broadcast advertisements on independent television. For example, it will censor advertisements that are likely to be offensive.

Inflation A situation whereby the value of money, in terms of spending power, declines. This occurs where too much money is chasing too few commodities.

Information Raw data that has been processed to produce meaningful knowledge and upon which decisions can be made.

Information processing The organising of information in useful ways. The processing may be carried out manually by people or by machines.

Information Technology Developments in microcomputers, word processors, electronic mail systems and communication technology which have made possible the electronic office.

Ink jet printer A printer that builds up characters and graphics from patterns (matrices) of tiny blobs of ink squirted on the paper. The quality of print so produced is normally higher than that from dot-matrix printers.

Input device A peripheral unit which allows data to be entered into a computer. Examples are a *light pen* and a *keyboard*.

Insolvency A situation where a person's or a company's liabilities to creditors exceed assets. Their debts are bigger than the worth of all their assets and they are therefore unable to pay all their creditors.

Insurance A method of protecting a person or company against financial loss as a result of events which may or may not take place, eg damage to, or theft of, personal and business assets, and also injury. See *Assurance*.

Integrated package A package usually combining a word processor, database, spreadsheet and communications program, sometimes with other applications.

Interactive Describing a program or system that requires input from a user, to which the computer responds with output that may call for further input (ie almost any program apart from one where the user simply gazes at the screen).

Interest 1. A fee charged for the use of borrowed money. 2. A financial stake in a concern.

Interest rate The particular amount of interest that will be charged for borrowing money. The rate is shown as a percentage.

Invoice A document that is sent by the supplier to a customer after goods or services have been provided. The invoice will list the products or services supplied, their prices and the total amount due.

IT See *Information Technology*.

Job description A document which literally describes the job. It would highlight the main tasks of the job and the responsibilities of the person doing it. A job description would normally be part of an employee's contract of employment.

Job enlargement Whereby extra tasks are added to a job in order to provide the job holder with a greater variety.

Job enrichment Workers are given greater scope in deciding how the tasks are to be performed. The range of tasks is extended vertically, to enrich the quality of the job for the worker.

Job rotation Whereby workers rotate around jobs in their department on a regular basis, to provide greater variety and increased job satisfaction.

Job satisfaction The satisfaction that an employee gains (or does not) from his/her job. It is generally accepted that employees who are satisfied with their jobs are more motivated and therefore more productive, compared with dissatisfied workers.

Job sharing A situation where a full-time job is shared (usually) by two people. For instance, one person may work in the morning and the other person in the afternoon. Alternatively, one person works the first two and a half days of the week and the other person works the latter two and a half days. Each partner is paid pro rata according to the number of hours worked. The participants share promotion and perks.

Joint account A bank or building society account opened in the name of two or more people.

Just in time A system of ordering stock or materials only as and when needed, just in time. The objective is to reduce stockholding to an absolute minimum, and cuts costs.

Keyboard (computer) An inputting device, which has a standard (QWERTY) typewriter layout with additional keys such as function, control and escape keys.

Kilobyte 1000 bytes (actually, 1024).

LAN See *Local area network*.

Laptop computer A small microcomputer which is portable and can be used on one's lap.

Laser printer A printer that uses laser light to produce an image. Laser printers are faster and quieter than earlier types of printer like the daisywheel or *dot-matrix*, and generally produce print work of higher quality.

Legal tender Money which a person is obliged by law to accept in payment of a debt.

Light pen An inputting device, usually for reading bar-codes.

Limited liability An arrangement, authorised by statute, under which a shareholder in a business cannot lose more than the amount paid for the shares.

Liquid assets Assets either in the form of money, or which can quickly be converted into money.

Liquidation In terminating or winding up a business, 'going into liquidation' means not only converting assets into cash but also paying all business debts. Once all debts have been cleared, any balance of cash can be distributed to the owners.

Local Area Network Where a number of computers are linked together, usually in the same room or building. Contrast with *Wide Area Network*.

Ltd The abbreviation used to denote a private limited company.

Macro instruction A source program instruction which, when translated, gives rise to several or many machine code instructions.

Magnetic disk A direct-access storage medium consisting of one or more flat circular disks, from which data can be retrieved directly without searching through other items of data which are not required.

Magnetic tape A tape with a magnetisable layer on which data can be stored.

Mainframe A term used to distinguish large and powerful computers from the smaller *minicomputers* and *micro-computers*.

Main memory The memory of the computer which stores programs and data currently being run (processed by the *CPU*). When power is turned off the data is lost.

Management functions These can be grouped into five areas: planning, decision making, organising and co-ordinating, leadership and motivation, and control.

Management levels Generally speaking, three levels can be seen in all organisations: top or strategic management, middle or tactical management and junior or operational management.

Marginal costs The extra cost involved in increasing output by an additional unit.

Market research The process of investigating customers and potential customers. It helps to identify why some people buy a company's products or services and some don't.

Megabyte One million bytes.

Megahertz (MHz) One million Hertz. Measures speed of *CPU*.

Memorandum (memo) An internal document used for communication. Normally used for giving information of a brief nature.

Menu (computer) A pull-down list of options from which the user can make a selection.

Menu-driven program A list of options presented by the computer. The user can make a selection from a *menu* by moving the cursor and then pressing the enter key, or by clicking on it with a *mouse*.

Microcomputer Usually refers to a third generation computer whose *central processing unit* is made up of a silicon chip which contains thousands of integrated microscopic electronic components housing the arithmetic and logic unit, plus the central unit. A small computer such as a personal computer.

Microprocessor A *central processing unit* (CPU) or co-processor contained on single chip.

Minicomputer A medium-sized computer, bigger than a *microcomputer* but smaller than a *mainframe*.

Minutes (of a meeting) A record of a meeting, ie what decisions were reached and what action, if any, and by whom, is to be taken. The minutes do not record the events of the meeting verbatim.

MIP Million instructions per second. This is a measure of *microprocessor* speed.

MIS Management Information Systems.

Mission statement This states briefly the main aims and objectives of the organisation.

Mixed economy Here the economy is partly 'free' and partly controlled by the state through the public ownership of certain industries.

Modem MOdulator/DEModulator. A device that allows *computers* to communicate with one another via a tele-communication line.

Money A medium of exchange, eg notes and coins.

Monitor The screen on which information is displayed, more commonly known as a *VDU* (Visual Display Unit).

Monopolies and Mergers Commission The government agency charged with the task of ruling whether a monopoly has been created and which imposes strict penalties on guilty parties.

Monopoly May be defined, in terms of economic theory, as where there is a single supplier of a product or service and no close substitutes. Thus the seller has complete control over the amount supplied and the price charged. However, there is a legal definition which would consider a business to be a monopoly if it controlled 25 per cent or more of a specific market. See *Monopolies and Mergers Commission*.

Mortgage A loan made against a property conveyed to the lender as security. The loan is usually provided for the purchase of a property over a long period, normally 20 to 25 years. In the past building societies were the major providers of mortgages; however, in recent years banks have also started to provide this type of finance.

Mouse A small hand-held device used for cursor control. Useful for selecting options (*icons*) in a *menu-driven program*.

Multinationals. See *Transnationals*.

Multi-skilling The training of employees to enable them to do several jobs rather than just one.

Multi-user system A system that allows several users to access the computer simultaneously.

Nanosecond One thousand millionth of a second.

National insurance A tax paid by both employers and employees to the Department of Social Security (Contributions Agency). The money is used to pay for such things as the NHS and state pensions.

Nationalisation A situation where the government takes over either a company or a whole industry and brings it within the public sector. For example, the different railway companies were taken over and British Rail (now privatised) was formed by the government.

Net profit The profit after all expenses have been accounted for. See *Gross profit*.

Network A number of computers linked together, with the capacity to share computing power or storage facilities.

NLQ (Near Letter Quality) Refers to quality of printing.

OECD Organisation for Economic Cooperation and Development.

Off line Not under the control of the central processor.

Oligopoly A situation where there are only a few sellers in the market, therefore competition is far from perfect, and prices tend to be kept high.

On line Under the control of the central processor.

Operating system A set of programs which supervise and control the general running of the computer.

Opportunity cost If you were to purchase a product for, say, £10, the opportunity cost is the cost of not being able to do something else with that sum of money, ie it is the items forgone.

Organisation This may be defined as a group of individuals interacting with one another to achieve predetermined aims or goals.

Organisation chart A diagrammatic representation of the official relationships and reporting levels, departments, levels of management and so on which make up the formal organisation.

Output device A device such as a printer that allows the computer to produce (output) information.

Overwriting Where a data item is written over an existing data item, which is erased as a result. For example, if a file is saved using the same name as an existing file, the new file will be saved and the existing one will be erased.

PABX Private Automatic Branch Exchange (telephone).

Partnership Where two or more people join together to form and run a business with the aim of making a profit. The maximum number of people that can form a partnership is 20.

Password A set of characters which must be presented to the computer before access is allowed either to the whole system or part of it.

PAYE Pay As You Earn. A system whereby tax is deducted from the pay of an employee at source.

Peripheral device Items such as printers, keyboards etc that can be connected to the *CPU*.

Person specification A document that is used during the recruitment and selection process for a job vacancy. The document specifies the personal qualities, attributes and qualifications required for the job.

Picosecond One million-millionth of a second.

Price determination At any time less of a good tends to be bought if the price is high than if the price is low.

Primary sector That part of the industrial sector which is concerned with extracting natural resources, for example mining, fishing and agriculture.

Private sector Where businesses are owned by private individuals, either wholly or as shareholders.

Privatisation A process whereby a company or an industry that is owned and controlled by the government is sold to the public through a flotation. Examples include British Telecom, British Gas, water authorities etc.

Prospectus A document issued by a company when it intends to sell shares to the public and other institutions. The document will detail the health of the organisation, ie its past performance and a forecast of its likely future performance.

PSBR Public Sector Borrowing Requirement. The amount of money that the government needs to borrow in order to balance its books. This is the difference between the revenue collected (from taxes etc) and the amount needed for public services such as health and education.

Public corporation A business which is wholly owned or controlled by the government either directly or indirectly, eg the BBC.

Public limited company A company which has limited liability and whose shares are traded on the Stock Exchange.

Public sector That part of the economy which is either owned or controlled by the state, eg the health service, education, Post Office.

Pull-down menu A facility whereby a user can 'pull' a menu down on to the screen by selecting an *icon* or a word from the top of the screen.

Race Relations Act 1976 An Act of Parliament which prohibits discrimination against people on the grounds of their race, colour, creed etc.

RAM Random Access Memory.

Red tape A term often used to refer to bureaucratic organisations in which rules stipulate in detail how the duties are to be carried out, and which are seen to inhibit flexibility and detract from effectiveness.

Redundancy The termination of an individual's employment when the job ceases to be required or where the employer ceases trading.

Registrar of Companies The official charged with the responsibility of maintaining a record of all limited liability companies (joint-stock companies). All these companies are required by law to lodge a copy of their Memorandum of Association and *Articles of Association* and annual accounts with the Registrar at Companies House.

ROM Read Only Memory.

Sale of Goods Act 1979 As far as customers are concerned, this Act requires sellers to ensure that the goods are of merchantable quality and fit for the purpose of their intended use. For example, a new umbrella would not be expected to have holes in it.

Scanner A device which can convert text and graphics into computer-readable form. For example, a picture could be scanned, which could then be displayed on the *VDU*.

Scroll When text either rolls up or down on the *VDU*. As each new line appears at the bottom of the screen, the lines at the top disappear one by one. Similar to credits at the end of a film.

Search The scanning of data items according to specified criteria, eg all names beginning with the letter M.

Secondary sector The part of industry in which raw materials are processed into manufactured goods, for example steel turned into cars and potatoes turned into chips.

Sex Discrimination Acts 1975 and 1986 The Sex Discrimination Act 1975 made discrimination on the grounds of sex or marital status in jobs, training and employment benefits unlawful. As well as direct discrimination, indirect discrimination, for example framing a job advertisement in such a way as to intentionally exclude women, is unlawful. The 1986 Act was passed in response to the European Court ruling, to remove the exemptions that existed for small firms and private household employers.

Simplex line A data transmission line which allows data to be sent in one direction only.

Soft sectored Refers to the way in which a disk has been formatted. Sectors are designated by information written on the disk by a program. The sectors can be altered.

Software Programs of various types which can be run on a computer.

Sole trader An individual running a business in his/her own name or other suitable trading name. Examples include a corner shop or a market trader.

Sort To arrange data in a particular order, eg alphabetically or numerically.

Sponsorship Whereby a company pays a famous sports personality or team to wear the company's logo or other brand name. Sponsorship is generally associated with sporting activities but not restricted to it.

Statutory Rights These are rights that are conferred on individuals by various Acts of parliament.

Strike A situation whereby the workers withdraw their labour as a protest. Reasons why a strike might be called are no wage increase or a small one, or threat of job losses.

SWOT Strengths, Weaknesses, Opportunities and Threats (analysis).

System A set of functions or parts that interact with one another to achieve a goal or objective, eg an organisation or a human body can be viewed as a system.

Systems analyst A person specialising in systems analysis.

Systems software Programs which are concerned with the running of the *hardware* and not with specific applications, eg utilities, operating systems.

Telecommuting A word that has come to mean employment where a worker does not have to travel to work, but is connected to the office or place of work via a computer terminal.

Teleconferencing This allows a number of people to be simultaneously connected by telephone so that discussion can take place even though they do not meet. They need not be in the same building or even in the same country. See *Videoconferencing*.

Teleworking See *Telecommuting*.

Tertiary sector An industrial sector in which service is provided rather than products, for example banking and insurance.

TQM Total Quality Management.

Trade Descriptions Act This act makes it illegal to describe goods in any way that is untrue or could mislead the public.

Trades Union Congress (TUC) A federation to which most unions are affiliated. The TUC represents the trade union movement in dealings with government, and formulates policy for the whole movement.

Trading Standards Office All local authorities have a trading standards office or department. The trading standards officers enforce laws regarding such matters as false descriptions, prices, some aspects of the safety of consumer goods, short weights and measures, sales of cigarettes to under 16s etc.

Transnationals Business organisations whose activities are conducted in several countries. Examples are Ford Motor Company, Philips, Nissan.

Variable costs These costs will vary in direct proportion to the level of production/activity of a firm.

Variance The difference between what was budgeted and the actual figures.

VDU Visual Display Unit. See *Monitor*.

Verification The act of ensuring that data transferred from source document to computer system is correct.

Videoconferencing Similar to *teleconferencing*, except that you have vision as well as sound.

Wide Area Network The linking together of computers in two or more separate buildings. Contrast with *Local Area Network*.

WIMP Windows, *icons*, *mouse* and *pull-down menus*.

Winchester disk A fixed disk drive in which a sealed unit houses the access arms and the magnetic disk. Also commonly referred to as a hard disk.

WORM Write Once, Read Many times.

Further Reading from Kogan Page

All You Need To Know About GNVQs: A Practical Guide For 14–18 Year Olds, Janet Gibson, 1996

Get Qualifications For What You Know And Can Do, Susan Simosko, 1992

Great Answers to Tough Interview Questions, 3rd edition, Martin John Yate, 1992

How to Pass A Levels and GNVQs, Howard Barlow, 3rd edition, 1995

How to Pass Computer Selection Tests, Sanjay Modha, 1994

How to Pass Graduate Recruitment Tests, Mike Bryon, 1994

How to Pass Numeracy Tests, Harry Tolley and Ken Thomas, 1996

How to Pass Selection Tests, Mike Bryon and Sanjay Modha, 1991

How to Pass Technical Selection Tests, Mike Bryon and Sanjay Modha, 1993

How to Pass the Civil Service Qualifying Tests, Mike Bryon, 1995

How to Pass Verbal Reasoning Tests, Harry Tolley and Ken Thomas, 1996

How to Succeed in Advanced Level Business GNVQs, Sanjay Modha, 1996

Interviews Made Easy, Mark Parkinson, 1994

NVQs and How to Get Them, Hazel Dakers, 1996

Test Your Own Aptitude, 2nd edition, Jim Barrett and Geoff Williams, 1990